PROLOG FOR COMPUTER SCIENCE

M. S. Dawe and C. M. Dawe

PROLOG
for Computer Science

Springer-Verlag
London Berlin Heidelberg New York
Paris Tokyo Hong Kong
Barcelona Budapest

M. S. Dawe
Department of Computer Science
University of Manchester
Oxford Road, Manchester, M13 9PL, UK

C. M. Dawe, PhD
Birch Tree House, The Street
Petham, Kent, CT4 5QU, UK

ISBN-13: 978-3-540-19811-6   e-ISBN-13: 978-1-4471-2031-5
DOI: 10.1007/ 978-1-4471-2031-5

British Library Cataloguing in Publication Data
A catalogue record for this book is available from the British Library

Library of Congress Cataloging-in-Publication Data
A catalogue record for this book is available from the Library of Congress

34/3830-543210 Printed on acid-free paper

Preface

As a computer language, Prolog is quite different from most others. It is one of the two languages which have generally been found suitable for artificial intelligence applications, and arguably the only one suitable for the study of natural languages. The range and versatility of these and other applications grows almost daily.

Prolog is a *logic programming language*, based on the principles of modern logic adapted to provide mechanical proof procedures. This does not mean that its applications are far-flung and of little practical significance, as a glance at the applications included in this book will prove.

The language is largely *declarative*, in that its programs aim to state the data structure of the subject area for which a program is being written, avoiding *procedural* aspects which are concerned more with the use of a computer. As a result Prolog can be learned with little knowledge of conventional computer programming.

As for any other computer language, many authors have written books about Prolog. Indeed, a list for further reading has been given as an appendix to this book. It was found by the present authors that, although excellent books were available, there was significant variation in style and emphasis. A general textbook providing a complete tutorial from basics, without over-specialisation, was lacking.

It is doubted whether today, a course in computer sciences could exclude Prolog. This book is intended for present and future generations of computer sciences undergraduates. It is also suitable for programmers who wish to extend their repertoire to include Prolog. It makes no pretence to be exhaustive or to develop a personal thesis. It does, however, cover a very broad range of topics both within and relevant to Prolog. There are many examples and questions, mostly paired with answers. No previous knowledge of computer languages is assumed. Nonetheless the reader should be able to establish an understanding of Prolog and sufficient fluency to attain acceptable grades in a diploma or degree course in computer sciences. This book will also provide an introductory course for those specialising in linguistics or artificial intelligence, who at the outset find the specialised texts too weighty.

After a brief introduction to Prolog's history and its differences from and similarities to other computer languages, there are fairly lengthy chapters on logic and logic programming. Although these chapters are more extensive than most Prolog books offer, they would still benefit from the support of a standard logic text. The intention of these chapters is for the reader to obtain some grasp of the fundamentals of logic. Logic and logic programming are subjects in their own rights and could not be covered fully in a volume such as this. However, we maintain that logic and logic programming are so intricately bound with Prolog that a mere summary would be insufficient. Not only this, but if better logic programming languages are to be developed, it is desirable that the basis upon which Prolog is built should be known. Another reason for the length of these chapters is to allow some time to be spent on what might be called *traditional* aspects of logic. When preparing a program, the programmer has to move from an account of the world given in natural and scientific languages, as well as, possibly, diagrams and so on, to what might be considered a Prolog *model*. The reader can benefit from some of the conclusions made by logicians undertaking such studies. It is worth remembering that no matter how much care is taken over the syntax of a program, the semantics have to be correct first.

Many readers will be impatient to get *hands-on* experience of Prolog. Despite what has just been said, the book has been written in such a way that it is still quite possible to skip the logic chapters, and return to them later. This will take the reader to chapter four, which introduces the main Prolog syntax.

In chapter five, the *goal searching* procedure by which Prolog reaches solutions to problems set by the user is explained, together with the ways in which it can be controlled.

Chapter six introduces the way in which Prolog handles arithmetic. This chapter is more extensive than would have been possible a few years ago, partly due to the increased number of standard mathematical functions now built in to more recent versions of Prolog. It is also due to the fact that the field of the underlying arithmetic now includes real numbers, rather than just integers, as was the case in early versions.

Chapter seven introduces the *built-in* commands available for text and file handling. These are especially important for Prolog, due to its enormous potential for interactive programming.

Information entered into Prolog can be expressed in a variety of formats. These and the ways they are processed are explained in chapter eight. *Lists, semantic networks* and *if . . . then . . .* rules are included. Some extensive applications and case studies are also presented.

In chapter nine, many of the errors which may occur in using Prolog are considered: the ways in which they can be detected and removed, or preferably avoided in the first place.

One of the first applications for Prolog was to the study of natural languages. The *parsing* process used is outlined in chapter ten. An English to Dutch translator is also included as a case study.

At least two philosophical questions come to light with a language such as Prolog. Given that it is called an artificial intelligence language, what does this mean? What should be expected from it? Also since one of the claims for Prolog is that its database states the structure of the real world more closely than those for other computer languages, do Prolog programs relate to the real world better than other languages at the observational level? In philosophical terms, how does the *empirical significance* of a Prolog program differ from that of programs written in other less declarative languages?

This book contains a wide range of applications from fields as diverse as linguistics, data-handling, planning, commerce, medicine and science. The applications provided by a computer language book are as important as the principles introduced. It is important to observe *how* Prolog is applied. Also, applied programs can often be used as the basis for more complex programs, without the need to consider all of the fundamentals.

At the back of this book is an extensive appendix. It includes a dictionary of predicates, a glossary of terms, common error statements, the ASCII codes, a list of operator precedences, availability of various dialects of Prolog, a table of debugging leashings, as well as a list for further reading.

Many people have helped us during the production of this book. Professor Wolfgang Balzer of Munich University first pointed out the existence of Prolog and checked the logic and philosophy chapters. Joseph Sneed of the University of Colorado helped with some of the philosophical aspects. Rachel Morton of Edinburgh University helped with some of our early misunderstandings of the language. David Morse of the University of Kent has been a constant oracle to consult. Alison Fowler of the University of Kent checked early drafts of the manuscript and gave us permission to use her Dutch to English translator program. Our referees have been of the greatest importance in the later stages of writing the book, especially Dr. Knott. Our thanks to David Warren at Bristol University for allowing us to include his Warplan program, to Burnham and Hall for permission to include the Insurance Quote program and to Chris Mellish of Edinburgh University for permission to use the travel agent program case studies. Last but by no means least, apologies to Janet, mother and wife, and David, brother and son for allowing us to see less of you, while we wrote the book.

M.S.D and C.M.D   Manchester and Petham
                                                                                          October, 1993

Contents

Chapter 1 · PROLOG

1.1	Why Learn Prolog?	1
1.2	Why Use this book?	2
1.3	Prolog	2
1.4	Limitations of Prolog	3
1.5	Past, Present and Future	4
1.6	Accessibility	5

Chapter 2 · LOGIC

2.1	Introduction	7
2.2	Traditional Logic	7
2.3	Symbolic Logic	11
2.4	Predicate Logic	17
2.5	Deductive Systems in the Real World	20

Chapter 3 · LOGIC PROGRAMMING

3.1	Predicate Logic for Prolog	21
3.2	Clauses in Predicate Logic	21
3.3	Resolution	23
3.4	Computation Rules	25

Chapter 4 · PROLOG SYNTAX

4.1	Entering Statements at Prolog's Command Line	27
4.2	Using a Text Editor to Write a Program	27
4.3	Comments	28
4.4	Terms	28
4.5	Predicates	29
4.6	Clauses	31
4.7	Variables	32
4.8	Logical Connectives	33
4.9	Rules	37
4.10	Empty Heads	38

4.11   Making Queries   39
4.12   Built-in Predicates   42
4.13   Operators   42
4.14   Declaring an Operator   43
4.15   Blank Variables   44
4.16   Equality   45
4.17   Recursion   46
4.18   Updating a Running Program   48
4.19   Lists   51
4.20   Applications   51

Chapter 5 · GOAL SEARCHING AND ITS CONTROL

5.1   Goals   55
5.2   Search Control   60
5.3   Extra Search Control Predicates   61

Chapter 6 · ARITHMETIC AND MATHEMATICS

6.1   Introduction   63
6.2   Arithmetic Predicates   64
6.3   Programs Using Arithmetic Predicates   66
6.4   Mathematical Functions   68
6.5   Mathematical Operations   70
6.6   Application   71

Chapter 7 · INPUT AND OUTPUT PREDICATES

7.1   User Interaction   73
7.2   write (term) and read (term)   73
7.3   get (Ascii), get0 (Ascii) and put (Ascii) ..   75
7.4   tab (I) and nl   76
7.5   name (atom, code)   78
7.6   Using Data Files   78
7.7   Controlling the Input and Output Streams ...   78

Chapter 8 · DATA STRUCTURES

8.1   Introduction   81
8.2   Lists   81
8.3   Operations on Lists   84
8.4   Semantic Networks   94
8.5   Frames   102
8.6   If . . . Then . . . Rules   107

Chapter 9 · PREVENTING AND REMOVING PROGRAM ERRORS

9.1	Introduction	117
9.2	Errors in the Modelling Process	117
9.3	Syntax Errors	119
9.4	Type Testing of Terms	120
9.5	More on Type Testing	122
9.6	Programming Style	123
9.7	Errors Due to Search Control	124
9.8	Debugging	126

Chapter 10 · NATURAL LANGUAGES

10.1	Parsing	131
10.2	An English to Dutch Translator	132

Chapter 11 · PHILOSOPHICAL ISSUES

11.1	Introduction	141
11.2	Machine Intelligence	141
11.3	Empirical Significance	143

Chapter 12 · PARALLEL PROCESSING PROLOG

12.1	Parallel Processing	147
12.2	Parallel Processing for Prolog	148

APPENDIX 1

Dictionary of Built-in Predicates 153

APPENDIX 2

Glossary of Terms 159

APPENDIX 3

Common Error Statements 165

APPENDIX 4

ASCII Codes 167

APPENDIX 5

List of Operator Precedences 169

APPENDIX 6

      Prolog Versions 171

APPENDIX 7

      Further Reading 173

APPENDIX 8

      Leashing Directory 175

REFERENCES 177

ANSWERS TO SELECTED QUESTIONS 179

INDEX 187

Chapter One
PROLOG

1.1 Why Learn Prolog?

New computer languages are developed every year. The computer science student might be expected to keep up with this increasing stock of languages. Therefore, it is obviously helpful to know at the outset, why a particular language is worth learning.

Many new languages are customised for specific applications. For example, a language might be more suitable for scientific applications, for teaching applications or for commercial applications. Such specialised languages could be invented, and refined *ad infinitum*. Prolog is not a new language in this sense. It represents a major departure in the way programming is practised. It is a fifth generation language, often written in, and making use of fourth generation languages such as *'C'* or *'Pascal'*. It is sometimes referred to as an *artificial intelligence language* and comes closer than its predecessors, to the way in which its human users think.

Learning a fourth generation language generally requires knowledge, of the way in which a program interacts with a computer. However, there are relatively few such distractions for Prolog. This is because Prolog is a more *declarative* language in which the programs predominantly *state* what the subject material of the program is, rather than a *procedural* one containing many *instructions* to the computer processor. As a result, what may be a lengthy and difficult program to write in a fourth generation language, might be much shorter and easier to write using Prolog. Indeed, powerful programs often run to just a few lines when written in Prolog.

Prolog is a *logic programming language*, making use of the principles of modern logic. To properly understand how Prolog works, some knowledge of logic and logic programming is required. Chapters on logic and logic programming are thus included, although these are only sufficient to provide an introduction to the subjects. The inclusion of a chapter on logic will also help the reader to appreciate the pitfalls which await the unwary, in preparing Prolog models of real life situations. The logic programming chapter may also interest the more ambitious who aspire to develop better logic programming languages in the future.

1.2 Why use this book?

The Prolog student is spoiled for choice when it comes to choosing a textbook. There are many books available, some of the best having been written by founding fathers of the language. We (the authors) came to Prolog as users. In connection with work on the logico-mathematico structure of genetics, it was decided to experiment with Prolog. At the outset it became apparent that in spite of all the books available, there is no easy-to-learn tutorial covering the language in great breadth, right from the basics. A book which would, in other words, at least acquaint one with Prolog at all relevant points, and which would also look at Prolog from the perspective of logic and logic programming. Existing books tend to develop their author's own interests and specialise on certain aspects or applications of the language. One result of this is that some aspects are dealt with in detail which is overwhelming for the novice. Another is that many important basic considerations are scarcely touched upon.

This book is primarily for undergraduate computer science students. Almost every aspect of Prolog included is supplemented with worked examples and exercises, most provided with answers. A wide and varied range of applications and case studies is included. Some of these are classics, some are new. They are drawn from commerce, science, medicine, law, mathematics and elsewhere. The book is thus a practical aid to learning Prolog.

However, this book includes many features which are usually absent elsewhere. For example, the modelling process which precedes actual programming is considered carefully, again with the use of many worked examples and exercises. There is discussion of some of the philosophical questions associated with the use of Prolog. To what extent is Prolog to be considered an artificial intelligence language? In what way does a Prolog program model the real world?

1.3 Prolog

One of the main applications for modern computers is modelling real world situations. The purpose of a programming language is to enable a computer to interpret commands which the programmer can comprehend with relative ease. An ideal computer language would be such that it could interpret purely declarative statements, without the need for any procedural statements. Prolog is far more declarative than other computer languages.

Although the process of converting a real life situation into a theoretical model might be carried out by scientists, mathematicians, economists, in fact by experts in any field, the logical principles used are the same. Over two hundred years ago, Leibniz conceived of a *calculator ratiocinator*, a system which would allow deductions about the real world to be made mechanically, analogous to arithmetic computation. Frege and Boole in the nineteenth century helped to provide the formal apparatus for this to be realised, and Russell developed the basis for present day *symbolic* logic at the beginning of the twentieth century.

Not until quite recently however, was an attempt made to design a computer language using logic. Many such varieties of a logic programming language are possible in principle. Prolog is actually short for *programming in logic*. It was first implemented in 1972 by Alain Colmerauer and Phillipe Roussel. Although many versions or dialects of Prolog are now available, all adhere quite closely to the *Edinburgh Prolog* developed by David Warren in the early nineteen-eighties. Prior to Prolog, the only accepted language for artificial intelligence applications was *LISP* and Warren was able to achieve speeds comparable with it using a compiler.

Prolog is not an ideal logic programming language, let alone artificial intelligence, language: The programmer cannot simply take a model of a real world situation and put it directly into a computer; there are still a number of procedural considerations. Prolog is nonetheless regarded as a fifth generation language, because of its comparative freedom from computer procedures during programming.

The decision whether to use *PROLOG* or *LISP* for artificial intelligence applications may rest on the personal preference and background of an individual programmer. However, the main influence on the use of PROLOG in recent years has been the decision of the Japanese government, to select PROLOG as the main language for its Fifth Generation Computer Systems Project.

1.4 Limitations of Prolog

In order to design a Prolog program, a real world situation has to be isolated. Relations and objects in the relevant domain can then be abstracted, and used to form the *data structure* or *knowledge structure* for a Prolog program. Ideally, the program is just the data structure. Sometimes, the knowledge structure with which the programmer starts will be self evident, or well-established. On other occasions, a great deal of pre-programming thought is needed in order to arrive at a suitable model for the situation.

The ways in which Prolog processes queries about that knowledge structure also have to be understood. If the program is not written correctly, the search process involved in answering a query may go wrong. For instance, it may run into loops and regress, the computer eventually running out of memory. Special built-in procedural facilities are available in order to minimise these problems.

Similarly, instructions are needed which enable a program to interface with the terminal, printer, and files etc. Other instructions allow the user to ensure that a display or print out is given in the most readable format.

Prolog was not originally designed to handle numbers. There are many computer languages for that purpose. Accordingly, early versions could only handle the standard arithmetical operators of addition, subtraction, multiplication and division. Furthermore there was the restriction that only integers could be used. Standard mathematical functions and operations were absent. Nonetheless with the powerful logical capabilities of Prolog, they could generally be user-defined. Alternatively, access to a library of functions or to a language supporting mathematical functions could be made. Most versions of Prolog nowadays operate with real numbers, including the integers, and have access to exhaustive libraries of built-in mathematical functions.

Compared to other computer languages, Prolog requires a large amount of computer memory in order to be implemented. This is due to the need to keep track of the search processes involved in answering a query. Such a large memory requirement was at one time considered a major disadvantage. However sufficient memory is now available even on home computers. Some earlier versions of the language, designed to operate with less memory, have thus largely fallen by the wayside.

A program written in Prolog consists of a set of rules representing a knowledge structure. Instead of giving the computer a set of individual commands to do something specific, a query is made about this data structure. Prolog then has to find a way to reach the answer or *goal*. The search procedure to this goal is carried out according to a set pattern, rather than by a random process. When a search along a certain route proves unsuccessful, Prolog will *backtrack* and search elsewhere, whereas other languages would usually show a run-time error.

The speed with which a version of Prolog operates is specified in *logical inferences per second (LIPS)*. The value of this varies widely between the different dialects and the machines which they are running on. If a compiler is used to convert the program first to machine code, the number of LIPS possible is much greater. Research projects have claimed up to 600 000 LIPS or 600 KLIPS and the figure is steadily rising. Compiled Edinburgh Prolog implemented on an improved DEC10 computer has been quoted to be 35-40 KLIPS. Today, even some home computers can exceed 20 KLIPS.

1.5 Past, Present and Future

Amongst the first applications of Prolog were those which used it to analyse and recreate natural languages. There have been extensive research applications in plane geometry, symbolic calculi, games theory, robotics and database management, to name but a few. Practical applications have mushroomed in recent years. They have seen light in travel agencies, statistics, architecture, drug design, library management, car engine fault diagnosis, carcinogenic activity studies, cardiac arrhythmics studies, house management, literature search and much more.

Prolog lends itself well to *expert systems*. In the future, such expert systems may be as common and as portable as hand-held calculators are today. They may help experts to check their decisions, especially when these have to be made in haste. Non-experts could also have access to urgent expert advice.

Developments in computer hardware, such as the increasing presence of parallel processors may well change the shape of logic programming, and of Prolog in years to come.

1.6 Accessibility

During the mid nineteen-eighties, fully-fledged versions of Prolog were only available on large expensive computers, situated in major institutions. However, there are many versions available now which will run on personal and home computers. At the same time, Prolog dialects for larger computers are becoming much faster, more powerful and more user-friendly.

This book cannot attempt to cover such a wide spectrum of developments. Today, a typical main-frame Prolog manual can run to four heavy volumes. Instead, a *core* version is provided which can be taken as the working basis for all alternatives, refinements and extensions.

Chapter Two
LOGIC

2.1 Introduction

Logic enters into the study of Prolog in at least two ways. First Prolog is an example of a logic programming language. Prolog was developed using the principles of modern symbolic logic. To understand the background to Prolog and the way in which it works, it is necessary to know at least some of these principles. Similarly a clearer understanding of the way in which Prolog operates, is a good basis for avoiding programming errors, and for clearing up troubles if they do occur. Second the path by which the real world is modelled and abstracted in preparation for programming is a treacherous one. A knowledge of logical principles will help this vital preparatory process. Therefore, no apology is made for spending some time on not only the principles of modern logic, but also some of the more traditional aspects.

In this chapter, only an outline of relevant features of logic can be given. Logic is a subject of its own and the reader intent on an in-depth study is recommended to refer to a logic text.

2.2 Traditional Logic

Logical *inferences* or *deductions* are made by us all on a daily basis. We assume for example, that a thing cannot both *be* and yet *not be*. This is a fundamental law of logic. By systemising logic, errors and inconsistencies in reasoning can be found. Logic states *laws of reasoning* which can be applied to *facts* which are already known.

There are two main branches of logic: *inductive* and *deductive*. As an example, deductive logic may involve arriving at some conclusion, given a general rule and a particular fact. Thus from the general rule *All men are mortal*, and the particular fact that *Socrates was a man*, we can deduce that *Socrates was mortal*. This form of *argument* originated over two thousand years ago.

Inductive reasoning is based on repeated instances. For example, from *Socrates was a man and died, Aristotle was a man and died, Plato was a man and died*, and so on, we might conclude that *all men die*.

There is a certain vocabulary used by logicians and which will be introduced throughout this chapter. Many of the words used are also in everyday use, and the technical meaning given to them by logicians must be distinguished in such cases.

A *proposition* is a statement of fact which can either be true or false. Thus *it is raining hard*, or *5 is a prime number* are propositions.

A *term* is a word or number, or a collection of these which form part of a proposition. *Raining hard*, or *5* are examples from the above propositions. Terms may be referred to as *positive* or *negative*. For instance *not raining* is the negative of *raining*. However, a mistake can easily be made here. It might be thought that *fine*, as in *the weather is fine* is the negation of *raining*. This is not so. There can be varying degrees of how fine it may be. The positive term and its negative must exhaust all possibilities. *Fine* would be a *contrary*, whilst *not raining* is the *contradictory*. Strictly, since a term only makes proper sense as part of a *sentence*, it is not the term, but the sentence which is negated. However the meaning of a sentence is often not made explicit, but is *understood*.

When modelling real-life situations, terms have to be *defined* clearly and correctly. One general approach to making definitions is to state the general type of entity and then to distinguish that which is to be defined from others of that type. Thus a *table* is a *piece of furniture* but it has a *flat surface*. Consider the definition of the term *schoolchildren*: *schoolchildren belong to the human race*. This definition is too broad, many others than schoolchildren belong to the human race. We can add that *schoolchildren are young*. This is better, at least fewer individuals would now be included by mistake. The more conditions that are added, the less chance there is of including an individual who is not actually a schoolchild. In general, as the number of conditions imposed increases, the number of individuals covered by the definition decreases.

Some aspects of a definition are there by the very nature of the object being defined. Thus with the definition *schoolchildren go to school*, it is a *necessary* property of schoolchildren that they go to school.

In defining a term, not only necessary conditions might be included, but *contingent* or *accidental* ones also. Thus if we take *schoolchildren wear uniforms*, this is not always the case for schoolchildren.

A definition must not contain the term which is being defined. Thus, *schoolchildren are schoolchildren between the years of five and eighteen who attend school* contains a statement which is always true, namely *schoolchildren are schoolchildren*. A statement which is always true is a *tautology*. This should not be confused with a *recursive* definition, in which a particular case of a term is defined in terms of an earlier case, but with some modification. Thus, the natural numbers might be defined: *The first natural number is 1. The nth natural number is the (n - 1)th natural number plus 1.* Recursive definitions appear later in the book and are frequently met in Prolog applications.

Double negatives should be avoided in a definition, and also single negatives where possible. Thus *it is not unfair* can be replaced by *it is fair*, provided that *fair* and *unfair* are contradictories. *It was a fair trial* is not necessarily the same as of *it was not an unfair trial*. The latter suggests that there was still some disagreement at the end of the trial.

A definition may be given by a *definite description*. For example *Sam and Sue are schoolchildren*. Or by *ostension*, (pointing). For example: *Those are schoolchildren*.

Another way to define a term is by *analogy*. For example: *College students are like older schoolchildren*.

Finally, it may not be possible to fully define a term. Nonetheless, by defining it with the help of of other less difficult terms, some progress could be made. Thus *religion is an idea*, swaps the problem of defining religion, for one of defining an idea, which may be less problematic.

If the meanings of terms used in a program are not defined correctly and adequately, Prolog programs will not model the real world situation correctly, no matter how much care is taken subsequently.

A *categorical* proposition asserts a fact as true or untrue. Traditionally, all propositions were thought of as being of *subject-predicate* form. For this, an object has a certain property or attribute, *predicated* of it. The *subject* is the entity being spoken about, and the *predicate* is a property which that subject has. Thus, *God is immortal*, takes *God* as the subject and *immortal* as the predicate.

A *hypothetical* proposition is *conditional* on some eventuality. Take the example: *If it is sunny later, I will go to the fair*. Here *it is sunny later* is the precondition or *antecedent* and *I will go to the fair*, the conclusion or *consequent*.

A *disjunctive* proposition expresses an *alternative*. For example: *At three o'clock I shall either go to the fair or I shall go shopping*. In this example the use of *or* is *exclusive*, since it is impossible for both events to occur. However, *or* may in some cases be interpreted as including *both* possibilities: We might say, *he could write or phone*. In this case he could do both.

A *dilemma* is a situation in which both possible outcomes are in some way unsatisfactory. Thus: *If I stay up late and study, I will be too tired in the morning to pass my exam, but if I don't stay up late and study I will not know enough to pass my exam* is a dilemma. The two unsatisfactory possibilities of a dilemma are its *horns*. However what may at first appear to be a dilemma might not actually be one. For example: *if I stay up late and study, I will be too tired in the morning to do well in my exam, but if I don't stay up late and study I will not know enough to pass my exam,* is not a dilemma, since to *do well* and to *fail* are not contradictories. You could choose to stay up late, since then you would stand the chance of passing your exam, even if you don't do well. This is a *rebuttal* of the dilemma.

Inference in natural language, including scientific natural language, is replete with possibilities for error in *logical fallacies,* and *invalid argument.* Some of these will be mentioned now. In *equivocation,* the same term is used in distinct ways. For example: *There should be no compromise on a matter of principle, the principle of moments is a principle, therefore there should be no compromise on the principle of moments.* Again, *grammatical ambiguity* may occur. Shakespeare wrote: *The Duke yet lives that Henry shall depose.* Does this mean that Henry will depose the Duke or that the Duke will depose Henry? Errors due to punctuation can occur. *The piano was sold to the lady with mahogany legs.* What is presumably meant is: *The piano was sold, to the lady, with mahogany legs.*

Sometimes, a general rule is wrongly applied to a special case. For instance: *Eating is good for you, therefore eating poisonous fungi is good for you.* Conversely, wrongly arguing from a special case to a general one leads to fallacy: *Socialising is good if it improves your character, so I will socialise with murderers since this will improve my character.* In this example, the qualification *if it improves your character* has been ignored.

The point at issue may be avoided. In an argument between two neighbours, one may say: *Please don't have your bonfire there, the smoke will blow into our lounge.* To this the other may respond: *Why not? Your tree overhangs our garden.* The point at issue was the bonfire and not the tree.

At times there may be the fallacy of *appeal to the populus.* A mother may say to her son: *You have to wear a tie to school, the school rules say so.* The son may retort: *None of my friends do!* Here, the point that obedience to the school rules is required, is answered by saying that many people do not obey the rules.

Arguing in a circle occurs when the conclusion to an argument includes the starting point: *I will be early, provided I catch the train, because it never arrives late.* A *regression* occurs where the general principle invoked needs proving as much as the original conclusion: *Increasing levels of asthma may be due to as yet unspecified pollutants in the atmosphere.*

Sometimes an affirmative or negative answer is demanded to a question which will not allow it. For example: *Have you stopped beating your wife?* If the answer is *no,* the implication is that he should stop beating her. If the answer is *yes,* the implication is that he has been.

Meaning is context dependent, not only for the terms as written, but also as used. Thus, a doctor may approach someone and ask: *Now, what seems to be the trouble?* The assumption is that the person is ill. If that person is not in fact the would-be patient, the query does not make proper sense.

Finally there is the fallacy of arguing from lack of understanding or the wrong cause: *No wonder they never have any money, he's always at the pub.* He might have a part-time job at the pub to earn extra money!

A valid method for deducing one proposition from another, is known as a *rule of inference* or a *rule of valid argument*. For example, the rule known as *modus ponens* and which is central to Prolog *proofs*, is applied in the following: *If James is a man, then James is mortal. James is a man. Therefore, James is mortal.* There will be more on such rules in the following section.

Traditional Logic Exercise

1. What are the fallacies in these arguments?

a) The people who park in our street when there's a cricket match on, are a nuisance. The Jones's always park in our street. Therefore the Jones's are a nuisance.

b) All that Alan, Beatrice and Christine ever do is watch television. It's no wonder that the younger generation are so badly disciplined.

2. Which pairs of words are contraries and which contradictories?

   a)   recent, ancient,
   b)   positive, negative,
   c)   greater, less,
   d)   add, subtract,
   e)   Londoner, Parisian,
   f)   physical, chemical,
   g)   legal, illegal.

3. Give definitions of each of the following:

   a)   post box,
   b)   hammer,
   c)   word processor,
   d)   computer program,
   e)   dog.

2.3 Symbolic Logic

Modern logic is able to deal with traditional concepts, but there is a shift in method and in emphasis.

Importantly, modern logic makes use of a special notation which can loosely be thought of as *algebraic*. It provides the logician with a rigorous means to carry out deductions according to accepted conventions. A logical statement is analysed into component propositions and the *connectives* or *logical constants* which relate them to each other. In *propositional* logic, each proposition is symbolised by a letter. Connectives use further symbols. Brackets are usually needed to assist in punctuation of the symbolised statements. Brackets may be needed in compound formulae involving more than one connective, in order to show *precedence*, the order in which connectives are to be evaluated. Provided a statement is punctuated correctly and intelligibly, it is a *well-formed formula*. Rules of inference are also needed to state what will count as valid deductions in arguments.

The intention is not however to symbolise the statements of natural or scientific language as they usually appear. Rather, essential features are abstracted in what amounts to a modelling process. Hopefully the *logical reconstruction* so produced, resembles the original in all important respects, but is simpler and more rigorous. Using such a *deductive system*, deductions can be made without recourse to the real world. The way in which such a system relates to the real world and thus gains *empirical significance* is discussed later in this book. A deductive system is *complete* if all valid arguments can be proven in it. It is *consistent* if use of the logical constants does not lead to a *contradiction* in which something is being held both to be and to not be the case. An *axiom* was traditionally defined as being a proposition which was *self-evident* and not in need of proof. For the modern logician, an axiom is thought of as a proposition which cannot be deduced from the other axioms of a *deductive system*. Strictly, this holds only if the axioms are independent of each other.

The logical connectives used in a such a *propositional calculus* are defined by *truth tables*. Two truth values are allowed, *true* (*T* or 1) and *false* (*F* or 0).

Negation is defined by the truth table:

p	$-p$
T	*F*
F	*T*

According to this truth table, a proposition is false if its negation is true, and true if its negation is false. However, for Prolog there is the assumption of a *closed world*. For this, negation of a proposition does not mean that the proposition is false but only that it is not true in the world which the proposition is currently addressing, the *universe of discourse*.

Conjunction is defined by:

p	q	$p\&q$
T	*T*	*T*
T	*F*	*F*
F	*T*	*F*
F	*F*	*F*

The conjunction of two propositions is only true if both propositions are true.

There are two forms of *disjunction*, both of which are covered by using the word *or* in natural language. In *weak* disjunction, both possibilities can occur. This corresponds to the inclusive use. It is this form of disjunction which symbolic logic and Prolog use. The truth table for weak disjunction *v* is given next.

p	*q*	*pvq*
T	*T*	*T*
T	*F*	*T*
F	*T*	*T*
F	*F*	*F*

The weak disjunction of two propositions is only false when both propositions are false.

There is also a *strong* disjunction corresponding to the *exclusive* use of *or* when both possibilities cannot occur. Although there is not a specific symbol for strong disjunction, it can be defined using weak disjunction and conjunction. Essentially strong disjunction of two propositions is a weak disjunction of the two propositions conjoined with the negation of the conjunction of the original two propositions:

$$(p \lor q) \ \& \ -(p \ \& \ q)$$

It may be required to symbolise that one proposition entails another. The *if...then...* statement for this purpose is difficult and easily misused. Consider the proposition: *If it is sunny tomorrow morning then it will rain later on.* This proposition is of an *if...then...* form. In modern logic it is symbolised using the *material implication*. Using *p* for *it is sunny tomorrow morning* and *q* for *it will rain later on*, we write $p \rightarrow q$. This is read as *if p then q* or sometimes as *q is implied by p*. A further variation is to have the arrow pointing from right to left. The material implication contains an *antecedent*, (the *premiss, p*) and a *consequent*, (the *conclusion q*).

Here is the truth table for material implication:

p	*q*	$p \rightarrow q$
T	*T*	*T*
T	*F*	*F*
F	*T*	*T*
F	*F*	*T*

The material implication is only false if the antecedent is true, and the consequent false.

The results of using the above truth table are at times not what would have expected from an *if-then* statement. Returning to the proposition: *If it is sunny tomorrow morning then it will rain later on.* If it is *false* that *it is sunny tomorrow morning* and *true* that *it will rain later on*, then *if it is sunny tomorrow morning then it will rain later on* is, according to the truth table, *true*. If the consequent is *true*, then so is the implication, no matter what the antecedent. Even more surprisingly: If *it is sunny tomorrow morning* is *false* and *it will rain later on* is *false* then *if it is sunny tomorrow morning it will be sunny later on* is true. A *false* antecedent and a *false* consequent gives a *true* material implication.

It must be appreciated that the material implication connective only covers some of the uses to which *if...then...* is put in natural language. If there is doubt as to whether it should be used for a particular case, refer to the truth table and make substitutions of truth values into the antecedent and consequent. See if the truth values of the implication come out as expected.

Material equivalence holds between two propositions when each materially implies the other. By using the truth tables already introduced, it is possible to arrive at the truth table for material equivalence, an approach known as the *method of truth tables.*

p	q	$p \rightarrow q$	$q \rightarrow p$	$(p \rightarrow q) \& (q \rightarrow p)$	$p \leftrightarrow q$
T	*T*	*T*	*T*	*T*	*T*
T	*F*	*F*	*T*	*F*	*F*
F	*T*	*T*	*F*	*F*	*F*
F	*F*	*T*	*T*	*T*	*T*

There is also *logical equivalence* $\equiv$. In this the truth value is always *true*. A logical equivalence is a thus tautology, and its negation is a contradiction.

By comparing the truth table for $p \rightarrow q$ with that for *-p v q,* it is seen that they are logically equivalent. Similarly, *-(p & q)* is logically equivalent to *-p & -q.* These results are important in the mechanical proof procedures used by Prolog.

Apart from the problems already mentioned, material implication may not allow for a *causal* aspect to an *if...then...* statement. There may be a cause and effect aspect to the situation described in a proposition. For example, *if it rains then the streets get wet.* Again, *counterfactuals* of the form *if...had happened then...* do not seem to be adequately defined either. There are also pitfalls to avoid in using other connectives. For example, using & to represent *they got married and had a child*, ignores the *commutativity* of &, so that *they had a child and got married* is also true.

The truth table method used previously to find the truth table for logical equivalence, lends itself to proving an argument to be *invalid*. A row of a truth table in which the premiss is true and the conclusion false proves invalidity. Fortunately, it is not necessary to go through all of the combinations of truth values to find this. In the *short-cut* truth table method, a choice of truth values is made which would make the premiss true, but lead to a false conclusion. For example, consider the argument:

$$p \vee (q \ \& \ \text{-}r)$$
$$p \rightarrow \text{-}r \ therefore \ r$$

p	q	$p{\vee}(q\&\text{-}r)$	$p \rightarrow \text{-}r$	r
T	T	T	T	F
|	|			|
premiss	premiss			conclusion

This argument is invalid, since it has true premisses and a false conclusion for some assignation of truth values.

If the number of propositions is large, greatly increased numbers of combinations of truth values will appear. Even the short cut method would take too long. A *truth tree* method is then used. This method is closely related to that employed by Prolog. Truth values of propositions already dealt with are used to restrict the possible combinations remaining. Effectively, the conclusion to an argument is denied and a set of truth values is then sought which will provide a *counter example*. If none can be found, then the original argument must have been *valid*.

Rules of inference from traditional logic, are in most cases taken over and developed in symbolic logic. For instance, the rule of inference *modus ponens* can be written:

$$p \rightarrow q$$
$$p$$
$$/therefore \ q$$

Symbolic Logic Exercise

1. Find by the truth table method which of the following are logically equivalent:
   a) *-p & -q* and *-(p & q)*,
   b) *-p v -q* and *-(p v q)*.

2. State whether the word *or* is used in an inclusive or an exclusive sense in the following:
   a) If you run or take your bicycle, you will get to the shop before it closes.
   b) Members may be accompanied to the dinner by a friend or relative.
   c) From the photograph it appeared that either the house had subsidence or that the photographer was intoxicated.

3. Express each of the propositions in the previous question in symbolic logic.

4. Given that the propositions *p* and *r* are true and that the proposition s is false, what is the truth value of each of the following?:

a) *p & r*,

b) *p v (r & -s)*,

c) *(p→ s) → r*,

d) *(p & r) & -s*.

5. Which of the following hypothetical propositions can be expressed directly using the material implication sign. Check each by substituting truth values.

a) If he passes his exam then I'm the King of France.

b) If I am the chairman then I am rich.

c) If he had worked harder then he would have passed his exams.

d) If Roger is taller than Frederick then he is taller than Alan.

6. Taking:

  p = the wind is from the south,

  q = the wind is from the north,

  r = it is hot,

  s = it is cold,

Symbolise the following:

a) If the wind is from the south then it is hot.

b) If the wind is not from the south then it is not hot.

c) If the wind is neither from the south, nor from the north then it is not hot.

7. Express the following compound propositions in symbolic logic:

a) If James does not win the cup then it is not the case that either Jack or Roger wins the cup.

b) If Anne likes the party then James does not like the party, but if James does not like the party then Shiela does like the party.

8.

a) Test by the shortened truth table and truth tree methods whether the following is a contradiction:

  (p→ (p→ q))→ (-p & q).

b) Test whether this argument is valid or invalid;

  ((p & q) → r)→(-(p & q) → -r).

c) Is this argument valid?

  p → (q→-r),

  p v r,

  therefore p→ r.

9. Remove the implication sign in each of the following in favour of the *v* and *&* connectives:

a) *p→ (q→ r)*,

b) *(p→ q) → r*,

c) *(p→ q) ↔ (q→ r)*.

10. Symbolise each of the following and then move the negation sign inward in the resulting formula:

a) Phillipa is not happy and smiling.
b) There is no-one at the University who believes that ignorance is bliss.
c) Not everyone thinks that Prolog is good for you.

2.4 Predicate Logic

In *predicate* or *relational* logic, the inner structure of a proposition is made explicit. In the proposition *Sidney is the father of Diane and Diane is the mother of Kelly*, specific predicates or relations such as *father of* can be considered more closely. *Father of* is a *dyadic* or two-place predicate which requires at least two objects: the father and the child. The objects which take up places in a predicate are *arguments*. In *first-order* predicate logic, once a predicate is defined it does not vary, although it may be redefined for a different domain. In particular, a predicate may not be an argument of another predicate. It is often wrongly stated that Prolog uses first-order logic.

A relation may be written *Rab*, where *a* has the relation *R* to *b*. This is written in *prefix* form with the relation preceding its arguments. A relation may also be written in *postfix* form as *abR*. A third alternative is to write it in *infix* form, as *aRb*. This is the form usually used in arithmetic. When the infix form is used, the relation is frequently referred to as an *operator*, although the word can also be used in prefix and postfix contexts. Instead of speaking of propositions in predicate logic, it is usual to speak of *formulae*. Other names used for relations and predicates are *functors* and *functions*. More strictly functions or predicates are composed of a function symbol or functor, followed by the arguments.

A formula such as *Rab* or *Rxy* is an *atomic formula*, since it cannot be further reduced, logically speaking. One basic component for a predicate logic are its *atoms*. These are formulae which do not include any logical connectives. If *S* is *sister of*, *a* is *Anne* and *c* is *Charles*, we can write *Sac* for *Anne is the sister of Charles*. *Sax* might symbolise *Anne is somebody's sister*.

Quantification concerns *generalisations* such as *all...are...* and *some...are....* The former, *universal quantification*, is written *(x)P(x)*. The latter, *existential quantification* is written ($\exists x)Px$. Here *(x)* and ($\exists x$) are known as the universal and existential *quantifiers* respectively. *P* signifies some predicate, while *x* is a *variable*. *P(x)* is known as a *propositional function*. An example of a universal quantification, is *all men are human*: *For all x, if x is a man then x is mortal*, or symbolically ($x)(Mx \rightarrow Tx)$. An example of an existential quantification is *some men are tall. There exists an x such that if x is a man then x is tall.* In symbols, ($\exists x)(Mx \rightarrow Tx)$. Such general propositions may contain more than one quantifier.

When a variable which is in the scope of a quantifier, is replaced by a constant, the quantified proposition is said to be *instantiated*, in that an *instance* has been given. A propositional function is neither true nor false, but gains a truth value by virtue of a specific instantiation. A variable which is not within the scope of any universal or existential quantifier is *free*, whereas one which is, is *bound*. In a deduction it is essential to keep track of which variables are free and which bound. A particular instantiation of a propositional function provides an *interpretation* or a *model* for it. Generally a given function will allow more than one interpretation. For example, *X is taller than Y* might be interpreted with *X* and *Y* as buildings, people, animals or whatever.

Rules of inference are needed to deal with quantification. *Universal instantiation* (*UI*) says that any substitution instance of a propositional function can be validly inferred from its universal quantification. An *existential instantiation* (*EI*) similarly states that there is at least one individual of which an existential quantification is true. UI and EI are important in the mechanical proof processes of Prolog.

An example of modus ponens can thus be symbolised:

(x)(x is a prime number $\rightarrow$ x is an integer)
3 is a prime number
therefore 3 is an integer.

Notice that instantiation (to *x = 3*) was necessary. Only in this way could the *matching* or *unification* take place which is implicit in the use of the rule. Modus ponens cannot be applied to variables since the truth values are indeterminate. If *x is a variable* were used in the second line, no truth value can be stated. Hence no truth value can be deduced from the first line, and the truth value of the last line cannot be known.   Two further rules using quantification are helpful in understanding the proof procedures used by Prolog, and are given here:

-($\exists$ x)(Px) is logically equivalent to (x)(-Px).

-(x)(Px) is logically equivalent to ($\exists$ x)(-Px).

To prove invalidity when there is quantification, it is assumed that a general proposition is equivalent to a combination of singular propositions. Invalidity can then be proved by showing that the corresponding singular propositions admit truth values which would lead to invalidity.

It is thus possible to deal with valid arguments involving propositional functions, and to use the rules of inference already available for singular propositions.

If *Rx* signifies that *x is a member of the Rogers family*, we can quantify *($\exists$x)(Rx & Sax)*, to read *there exists an x such that x is a member of the Rogers family and Anne is the sister of x*. If *Fy* signifies that *y is female*, we write *($\exists$ x)($\exists$ y)(Fy & Rx$\rightarrow$ Syx)* which reads *there exists an x and there exists a y, such that if y is female and x is a member of the Rogers family,* *then y is the sister of x.* In this last example, the generality of a relation has been limited by a conditional, and this is a *rule*.

Relations have a number of properties. Only two-place relations will be considered here. A *symmetrical* relation is such that if one individual has that relation to a second, then the second has it to the first. In other words, it is *commutative*. Symbolically, *(x)(y)(Rxy → Ryx)*. *Cousin of* is an example. By contrast, an *asymmetrical* relation is such that if one individual has that relation to another, the second does not have it to the first. In symbols, *(x)(y)(Rxy → -Ryx)*. *Parent of* is an example of such a relation. A *nonsymmetrical* relation is one which is neither symmetrical nor asymmetrical.

A *transitive* relation is such that if one individual has it to a second, and the second has that relation to a third, then the first individual will have it to the third. It is symbolised as:

$$(x)(y)(z)((Rxy \ \& \ Ryz) \rightarrow Rxz)$$

Rxy could be *is greater than.*

A relation may also be *reflexive*, when any individual has that relation to itself. One symbolisation of this is:

$$(x)Rxx$$

An example would be *equals*. An *irreflexive* relation is one which no individual could have to itself. This could be symbolised as:

$$(x)-Rxx$$

An example would be the relation *is less than*. A *nonreflexive* relation is neither reflexive nor irreflexive.

Specific relations may have more than one of the above properties. For example, *same as* is symmetrical, transitive and reflexive.

Predicate Logic Exercise

1. Which of the properties of relations do each of the following possess?
    a) taller than,
    b) father of,
    c) brother of,
    d) ancestor of,
    e) two-way route to,
    f) predator of,
    g) married to.
2. Write each of the above using prefix, postfix and infix notations.
3. Use quantifiers to symbolise each of the following:
    a) All horse-riders are in danger.

b) Some motorists drive too fast.
c) All horse-riders are in danger because some motorists drive too fast.
d) If all motorists did not drive too fast then some horse-riders would not be in danger.

2.5 Deductive Systems in the Real World

It is important not to lose sight of the fact that logic gains its meaning, through interpretation in the real world. Scientific theories and other knowledge structures are sometimes optimistically claimed to be deductive systems, with well-defined logical structures. When modelling the real world in Prolog, there is the belief that at least the important aspects of reality can be treated in this way. Models representing objects and relations between them then provide a basis for inference using valid forms of argument.

Some disciplines such as Euclidean geometry, have been reconstructed with logical rigour, starting with axioms, and deriving *theorems*. However, this programme has not been applied widely. Part of the problem is the practical difficulty involved in expressing mature scientific disciplines in symbolic logic. There are questions about the way in which such deductive systems are to be related to the real world, and given empirical significance.

Furthermore although deductive systems must be complete and consistent, representations of the real world are often, or in a sense always, incomplete, inconsistent, or both. This is due partly to the process of abstraction which has to be employed in order to arrive at workable models of real life situations. It may also be desirable to leave a representation to some extent inaccurate or vague reflecting the existing state of knowledge in an area and leaving room for refinement.

However much such considerations have concerned philosophers and logicians, they have not deterred computer scientists as the bulk of this book will show.

Chapter Three
LOGIC PROGRAMMING

3.1 Predicate Logic for Prolog

In this chapter a brief outline is given of the way in which predicate logic is used to provide the mechanical proof processes used by Prolog. Logic programming and even the logical basis for Prolog are substantial subjects in their own right. The interested student will want to read specialised books on these. Some suitable books are cited in the reading list at the end of this book.

3.2 Clauses in Predicate Logic

For Prolog, the predicate calculus is modified. First, Prolog is not restricted to first order statements. Second, all formulae have to be expressed as *Horn clauses*. A Horn clause can be visualised at this stage as a material implication in which the consequent is a logical atom. This may at first appear to be extremely restrictive, and indeed Horn clauses do place some limitations on what can be said. These are not so serious as may at first be thought however. The restriction to Horn clauses is essential since it greatly simplifies the mechanical proof process for Prolog.

In order to be expressed as Horn clauses, formulae are first expressed in *clausal form*. To understand this concept, it is necessary to first explain what are called *literals*. A literal is an atom or a negated atom. A clause is then a disjunction of literals, with any variables present universally quantified. A clause might be, for example:

$$(x)(y)(F(x) \; v \; {-}G(x,y) \; v \; G(y,y))$$

A formula in predicate calculus may be written using only the connectives &, v and -, together with statement variables. The process of translating to clausal form is as follows: Implication is removed in favour of - and v. Occurrences of - are moved inward so as to apply only to atomic formulae. Quantifiers are removed by instantiation to *Skolem* constants. Effectively this is universal or existential instantiation. Quantifiers are moved left or removed completely. Finally & is distributed over v throughout the formula.

Consider the proposition: *If someone attends school, then they are a pupil.* This can be written using the material implication as:

$$(x)(Sx \rightarrow Px)$$

However, using the rule that,

$$P \rightarrow Q \quad \equiv \quad -P \vee Q$$

it can also be written as:

$$(x)(-Sx \vee Px)$$

Now consider the proposition, *There is no one who attends school, and is not a pupil.* This can be symbolised:

$$-(x)(Sx \ \& \ -Px)$$

Using the result that,

$$-(x)(Px) \quad \equiv \quad (\exists x)(-Px)$$

it can be written:

$$(\exists x)(-(Sx \ \& \ Px))$$

In this way the negation has been moved inward.

Using the rule that,

$$-(P \ \& \ Q) \quad \equiv \quad -P \vee -Q$$

it can further be written as:

$$(\exists x)(-Sx \vee -Px)$$

By existential instantiation, the variable in this example would next be replaced by an arbitrary individual. For example: *If someone attends school then they are a pupil,* becomes: *If any individual John attends school, then he, John, is a pupil.* Here Prolog assigns a unique number to each variable as its *Skolem constant.* More precisely, given a set of sentences containing constants, functions and predicates, the set of terms without variables, and only using constants and functions, can be arrived at. This is called the *Herbrand Universe.* The terms included are the *ground terms. Herbrand models* for some set of sentences are those which are true, when interpreted in the Herbrand Universe.

As a result of this process, the quantifier becomes superfluous for an existential quantification. However, for universal quantification a function is required which will state how the variable is related to real world entities.

The next stage is to move any universal quantifiers to the left of the formula, using the rules that

$$(x)(-Px) \quad \equiv \quad -(\exists x)(Px)$$

and

$$(\exists x)(-Px) \equiv -(x)(Px).$$

When a formula is in clausal form it is a collection of clauses, each of which is a collection of literals. The rules,

$$(P \& Q) v R \equiv (P \& Q) v (P \& R)$$
$$(P v Q) \& R \equiv (P \& R) v (Q \& R)$$

are usually needed to finally arrive at a clausal form.

When the propositions: *if someone attends school then they are a pupil* and *There is no-one who attends school and is not a pupil* are conjoined, the result is already in clausal form, with,

$$(-Sj \, v \, -Pj) \quad and \quad (\, -Sj \, v \, P(Fj))$$

as its clauses, instantiated here and with Fj representing the function needed because of the universal quantifier.

The literals of the first clause are $-Sj$ and $-Pj$ both negative. The literals of the second clause are $-Sj$ negative and $P(Fj)$ non-negated.

The clause $-Sj \, v \, P(Fj)$ could be converted back to a material implication, as $Sj \rightarrow P(Fj)$. Similarly, $-Sj \, v \, -Pj$ becomes $Sj \rightarrow Pj$. It is as an implication that such clauses are actually used by the Prolog programmer, since they are intuitively more accessible in the implication form.

3.3 Resolution

Once the deductive system is in clausal form, a rule of inference known as *resolution* can be applied to achieve mechanical theorem proving. To prove that some conclusion is entailed by some set of facts it is possible to prove that the conjunction of the negated conclusion and those facts gives a contradiction. For example, to know whether *it is raining out* implies that *the streets are wet*, ask whether *it is not the case that the streets are wet and it is raining out* is self contradictory. In resolution, the negated conclusions are added to the sets of given facts and the results checked for inconsistency.

Consider if two sentences are of the form,

$$A \& B \& ... \rightarrow G \, v H \, v ... \quad (1)$$
$$L \& M \& ... \rightarrow A \, v P \, v Q \, v ... \quad (2)$$

then if A is true it can be removed from the left hand side of *sentence (1)* and if it is false it can be removed from *(2)*. One way or the other, A can be removed to get:

$$B \& ... \& L \& ... \rightarrow G \, v H \, v ... \, v P \, v Q \, v ...$$

Provided all variables in the sentences are universally quantified, resolution is achieved by first unifying the sentences so that one atom is the same in both sentences. This is then removed from the combined sentences.

For example consider,

$$(x)(y)(B(F(x)) \& C(y) \rightarrow A(x)) \quad and$$
$$(z)(w)(D(G(z)) \rightarrow B(z) \& C(w))$$

Here, $B(F(x))$ will *unify* with $(z)F(x)$. This term can therefore be removed to get the combined sentence:

$$(x)(y)(w)(C(y) \ \& \ D(G(F(x)))) \rightarrow \!\!\!\!\!\!/ (x) \ v \ C(w))$$

If the same atomic formula appears both on the left hand side of one rule and on the right hand side of another, then the clause obtained by fitting them together and missing out the duplicated formula, follows from them.

In a Horn clause, literals on the left hand side of the $\rightarrow$ sign should not match up with more than one literal on the right hand side. In general, writing sentences in clausal form makes them long-winded and difficult to understand. Restricting them to Horn clauses in which there is only one consequent minimises these difficulties. Thus the sentences,

$$A \ \& \ B \ \& \ ... \rightarrow \ F \ and$$
$$P \ \& \ Q \ \& \ ... \rightarrow \ A$$

can be resolved to:

$$B \ \& \ ... \& \ P \ \& \ Q \ ... \rightarrow \ F$$

Because of this restriction, it is not possible to directly use Prolog to say, for example, *all objects are animate or inanimate,* since the conclusion *are animate or inanimate* is not an atom. An alternative formulation must be used.

Resolution is based on *proof by contradiction.* We start by asking: *Do there exist instantiations of the variable which make a formula true?* This is negated to: *For all instantiations, the formula is false.* Effectively if by resolution an *empty implication* is deduced, this is taken as *false,* making the original formula *true.* For example, let $F(x,y)$ mean *x is the father of y.* Given:

$$F(Sidney, Chris).$$

If it is intended to show that *Chris has a father,* we claim, as what in Prolog would be called a *goal,* that:

$$(\ \exists \ x)F(x, Chris)$$

This is negated to,

$$(x) \ -F(x, Chris)$$

and written as a Horn clause as:

$$F(x, Chris) \rightarrow (x)$$

Now a contradiction follows from,

$$F(sidney, Chris)$$

and

$$F(x, Chris) \rightarrow (x).$$

Unifying x with Sidney and resolving leaves the empty implication.

This contradicts the negation of the original goal, so that it can be validly deduced that *Chris has a father*.

More generally, clausal forms giving rise to,

$$(P1 \vee P2 \vee P3 \vee ...) \vee (-Q1 \vee -Q2 \vee -Q3 \vee ...)$$

are equivalent to,

$$(P1 \vee P2 \vee P3 \vee ...) \vee -(Q1 \& Q2 \& Q3 \vee ...)$$

which are equivalent to,

$$Q1 \& Q2 \& Q3 \& ... \rightarrow P1 \vee P2 \vee P3 \vee ...$$

Restriction to one unnegated literal of P1, P2, P3, ..., leads to,

$$Q1 \& Q2 \& Q3 \& ... \rightarrow P1$$

which is the Horn clause.

There are a number of ways in which Prolog varies from the above. For Prolog, matching of formulae is not quite the same thing as the unification process of resolution. It allows the case where a term matches up against a subterm of itself. In logic, such confusions of *type* have led to difficult *paradoxes*. However, there are only occasional difficulties with this in the normal range of Prolog applications. Furthermore, the definition of predicates in Prolog is an *if and only if* process. A program must first have all of its predicates transformed to this form. Another point to note is that in Prolog any *missing* predicates are given a negative definition.

3.4 Computation Rules

The mechanism for resolution and providing the empty $\rightarrow$ remains to be mentioned. This, the *computation rule* may take many forms in principle. In Prolog a *left-most* atom is selected first. However, the way in which the *matching* process then proceeds is still open. Due to the sequential mode of operation of most processors it is usually *depth-first*.

The differences between a depth-first search and a *breadth first* search can be visualised with the help of a *search tree*. (See Fig. 3.1). In a depth first search, as each *subgoal* is reached, the search proceeds to ever greater detail within that goal. If the nodes of the diagram, where lines branch, are taken as goals and subgoals, a depth-first search will start at A, move to B then to C and finally to D. It will then backtrack via C to E. It will backtrack again to F via B. From there the search will move to G. Again the search will backtrack, this time to H via F. The right hand branches of the search tree are now completed and the search returns to A. The process is now repeated for the right hand branches of the search tree.

For a breadth-first search, each branch is taken to the same depth in parallel. A disadvantage of the depth-first search is that it may not terminate, and enter a loop. This problem is not met with breadth-first search, but the architecture of most sequential processors does not lend itself well to this strategy. Referring to Figure 3.1. The search starts at A and moves to B. It then restarts at A and goes to I. Now it starts at B and goes to C. It starts again at B and goes F. Next the search goes to I and moves on to J. It returns to I and goes to K. The search now returns to C and goes first to D and then to E. It moves to F and goes first to G and then to H. On to J and then L and M. Finally to K and then N and after this O.

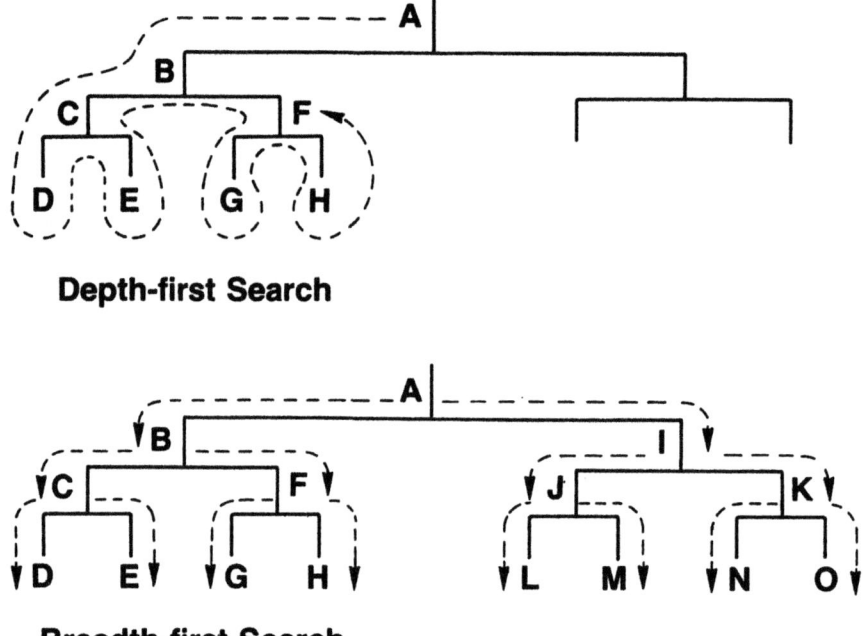

Depth-first Search

Breadth-first Search

Figure.3.1

Neither of these search strategies take account of the form of the search tree. It is possible to design more sophisticated strategies which will. These may result in finding a match for a specified goal more quickly in some pre-ordained problem area.

Chapter Four
PROLOG SYNTAX

4.1 Entering statements at Prolog's command line

The usual command line prompt for Prolog is something similar to:

```
?-
```

This implies that Prolog is waiting to be asked a question about its database. The examples in this book will include this prompt for convenience, so that they relate more closely to what can be seen on the screen. If an example does not contain this prompt, it is usually because an assertion is being made, and not a query. In this case, use the command consult or a text editor, as explained in the following pages.

Initially, Prolog will not have a database, and so one will have to be programmed. To enter the correct mode for asserting facts, enter:

```
?- consult(user).
```

or alternatively

```
?- [user].
```

In this mode the Prolog prompt is no longer ?-, because it is not expecting you to query any data. It is important to remember that the above command has a full-stop suffix. This is required for Prolog to understand that you have completed your command. To return to the query prompt, type:

```
end_of_file.
```

With some versions of Prolog, it is possible to use the end of file character (hold down Ctrl whilst pressing D or Z depending on the version of Prolog being used).

In order to return to a program to update it, Prolog responds to:

```
?- reconsult(user).
```

4.2 Using a text editor to write a program

In addition to entering data at the command line, it is possible to write a program with a text editor. Users of PCs will find such a utility with their version of DOS. Unix users and other machine owners should be able to get hold of one with little difficulty.

Facts can then be entered line by line on screen, and edited at will. To make queries of Prolog's database, the query prompt ? - will have to be added to the beginning of the relevant commands.

Unfortunately, due to the vast range of text editors available, it is not possible to give details of loading, editing and saving procedures individually. For these, the relevant manual will have to be seen.

To load and run a program written using a text editor, the following instruction can be used, at the Prolog command line:

```
?- consult(filename).
```
or
```
?- [filename].
```

filename is the full filename of the Prolog program. Here is an example for users of the *DOS* filing system: To run a program GENIUS, saved in a directory PROLOG on drive C, the following might be entered:

```
?- consult(c:\prolog\genius).
```

4.3 Comments

It is good practice when programming, to include comments about the effects of individual groups of instructions. This makes programs easier to debug and to develop. Other people will also be able to understand them more easily.

```
/*this is a comment*/
```

This is an example of a comment. Prolog will ignore the words this is a comment. Alternatively, this form may be used:

```
% so is this
```

Prolog will ignore everything to the right of the % symbol on that line.

Another use for comments is in providing a numbering system for clauses, useful for lengthy programs.

4.4 Terms

The building blocks for representing data in Prolog are called *terms*. They can represent variables, integers and real numbers, atoms and lists, all of which will be explained in due course.

Atoms are used to identify data, programs, files, and more. There are four kinds of atom. All of them designate constants, and can be over two hundred characters long. Alphanumeric atoms such as denim_jeans, start with a lower case letter and are followed, if required, by alphabetic characters (A - Z, a - z), digits (0 - 9), or underscores (_). Here are some examples of alphanumeric atoms.

```
banana        c3                banana_split
branch23      timeTable         alan
p_RS          employee_327_salary_group_D
```

Quoted atoms such as 'Denim Jeans' consist of any sequence of characters, enclosed in single quotes. By this means, proper nouns can be properly begun with capital letters, and an underscore does not have to be used between the words of an atom. The following are all legitimate quoted atoms.

```
'Banana-split is for dessert.'
'456'
'Hi user! What''s the problem?'
```

Notice that in the last example, two quotes have had to be used in the word where grammar dictates the use of an apostrophe. In some versions, it may not be possible to include apostrophes within an atom, because of their role in Prolog syntax.

A further kind of atom is the *symbolic* type. These are drawn from the characters of the upper half of the ASCII table (see appendix), and are:

```
#   $         &   =
-   ^         ~   \
@   '         :   .
/   +         *   ?
<   >
```

Combinations of the symbolic atoms are themselves atoms:

```
&&        $:      +->
```

Finally, there are the *special* atoms:

```
!       ;       [       ]
```

These are special in the sense that they are reserved for Prolog syntax.

Integers are constants, as are all real numbers. Although early versions of Prolog were confined to using positive integers, this is usually no longer the case. The use of real numbers in Prolog can occasionally result in inaccurate calculations, due to number rounding techniques which may be present.

Note that if numbers are enclosed in quotes, they are treated as atoms, and cannot be used for arithmetic.

4.5 Predicates

A *predicate* is the name given to a relationship holding between atoms or variables. There are *user-defined* predicates and *built-in* predicates. The available library of built-in predicates will vary with the version of Prolog being used. Those used in this book represent a core which is available on almost all versions. For details on version specific predicates, the reader should refer to the relevant Prolog handbook. A dictionary of built-in predicates is included as an appendix, and will be found useful as a quick-reference. Built-in predicates are also given a fuller explanation, in the relevant sections of this chapter.

The subjects of a predicate are its *arguments*, and the number of arguments to which a predicate applies is its *arity*. Predicates with no arguments occur, as will be seen later.

Predicates Examples

A predicate is written in the form of its name in lower case, followed by its arguments written in single brackets and separated by commas. Thus:

```
cousin(X, dave).
```

might be interpreted as *X is the cousin of Dave*. Again:

```
prime_number(3).
```

might be interpreted as *3 is a prime number*.

```
route(london, leicester, leeds, motorway).
```

might be interpreted as *there is a motorway route from London to Leeds which passes through Leicester*.

The names cousin, prime_number and route are usually referred to as the predicate's *functors*.

Often, predicates are named in the form predicate/arity. The functor route could then be written as route/4. Prolog usually refers to predicates in this way, when sending messages to the user. It is essential to use this form of naming, when more than one predicate with the same name, but different arity is present in a program.

When predicates are entered, the spaces between the arguments are ignored, and variations in this respect will not cause problems with the runnning of a program. Accordingly:

```
cousin(X, dave).
```
and
```
cousin(X,dave).
```

are the same thing to Prolog. The chosen format will depend whether it is conciseness or legibility that is more important to the programmer.

Prolog is indifferent as to whether whole words or just letters are used for the names of predicates and predicate arguments. However, a program will be more easily understood when words which relate clearly to the real world are employed. (For instance using cousin is more transparent than c, and david more so than d.) On the other hand, there is a case for abbreviation when using lengthy names, in order to save on programming time.

An alternative syntax for a relation between objects is given by the use of *operators*. These may be of the prefix type, where the functor precedes the variables:

```
father(chris, david)
```

or the *postfix* type, where the functor follows the arguments:

```
(chris, david)father
```

or again the *infix* type, where the functor is between the arguments:

```
(chris)father(david)
```

Arithmetic operators are usually written in the infix notation:

```
2 + 3
(X - Y) / 5
```

Depending on the actual relation being symbolised, one type may be easier to understand. Thus, using the previous example, the infix notation brings the meaning of the sentence *Chris is the father of David* across more clearly than the prefix or postfix types.

More often than not, however, the usual prefix predicate form is used. This is partly due to convention but also because when another type is to be used, its introduction is slightly more complicated. Nonetheless, there are many situations in which it is desirable to use the infix or postfix notation.

4.6 Clauses

To create a database, it is necessary to use clauses. These present information to Prolog, in ways which can be easily interpreted by the language. Here is an example of one:

```
clothing(denim_jeans).
```

might be intended to tell Prolog that *denim jeans are a form of clothing*. In this example, the clause is actually also the predicate clothing, because all that the clause contains is this predicate. However clauses can contain more than one predicate, as well as conditionals.

A clause must be terminated by a full stop . before entering When a collection of clauses define the same predicate, that collection of clauses is known as a *procedure*.

Clauses Examples

Here are some examples of English statements, translated into Prolog:
1. The letter a is a vowel.
    ```
    vowel(a).
    ```
2. The number 3 is a prime number.
    ```
    prime_number(3).
    ```
3. Chris is the father of Martin.
    ```
    father_of(chris, martin).
    ```
    or alternatively:
    ```
    father_of('Chris','Martin').
    ```
4. Mr. Edward John Allen lives at 52 Dixon Road, London, N.W.3.
    ```
    personal_fact('Allen,Edward John','52 Dixon
       Road','London','N.W.3').
    ```

Note that if for example, an alphabetical sorting procedure was to be applied to such clauses, the use of quotes would present difficulties. In such a case it would be desirable to enter at least the surname without quotes:

```
personal_fact(allen,'Edward John','52 Dixon Road,
   London,N.W.3').
```

Clauses Exercise

Write each of the following facts in Prolog, defining any terms and predicates used:
1. Prolog is a computer language.
2. I am learning Prolog.
3. The 09.40 train from Euston stops at Doncaster and terminates at Leeds.
4. ACME Manufacturing employs:
    127 fitters, 35 mechanics, 8supervisors, 2 shop floor managers and 1 production manager.
5. BGM supplies Smiths with stationery.

4.7 Variables

A variable is a quantity which is free to change. It was seen earlier in this chapter that constants cannot begin with capital letters, unless quotes are used. This is because names starting with capital letters are used to signify variables. Names starting with an underscore are also taken to denote variables. Thus the following are variables:

```
X
_tape_number
Age
```

When Prolog deals with variables, it actually changes them into constants by substituting constant values from a database, or by giving the variable a unique number. This process of substitution is called instantiation and was discussed in the logic chapter. When clauses are written containing variables, generalisations can be made from them.

The statement, *Prolog exists* can be written using the predicate exists as:

```
exists('Prolog').
```

This assertion contains only constants, but by using variables it is possible to widen its perspective. *Everything exists* could be translated into:

```
exists(Everything).
```

or:

```
exists(_everything).
```

where Everything or _everything is the variable. An instantiation of the variable Everything could be to the constant prolog or 'Prolog'.

In some programs, it may be desirable to deliberately instantiate a variable, for instance, when there is the likelihood of ambiguity. There is actually a built-in predicate numbervars which will do this. Thus if numbervars(Variable) is used, Prolog might assign the unique number 516 to Variable.

4.8 Logical Connectives

Prolog adopts, and adapts the logical connectives of predicate calculus. Their logical basis has been discussed in previous chapters, but they are listed here:

Nearest English word	Meaning	Prolog syntax
and	conjunction	,
or	disjunction	;
not	negation	not
if a then b	conditional	b :- a

The possibilities for ambiguity and error in using logical connectives have been discussed in the chapter on logic. These problems are inherited by Prolog, which adds some its own. It is strongly recommended that such limitations are understood.

In particular, there are two points concerning negation. Firstly, *not* does not obey the truth table of symbolic logic. The design of a program will often have to be a great simplification of the real world, by excluding external factors. Otherwise there will be too many factors to be taken account of. Accordingly *not* is to be taken as *not in the present universe of discourse* or *not for the given data structures*. There is a *closed world* assumption. It does not mean *false* in any absolute sense. Second, if *not* is applied to a variable in Prolog, an *error* is produced. This problem has been overcome in some versions of Prolog, by the introduction of a second *not* predicate, namely \+. This predicate will simply negate when applied to a variable.

Logical Connectives Examples

Assert:

```
retailer(smiths).
retailer(bhs).
wholesaler(bgm).
wholesaler(direct).
manufacturer(acme).
manufacturer(bosfit).
manufacturer(bgm).
```

These clauses are intended to assert that:

Smiths are retailers
BHS are retailers
BGM are wholesalers
Direct are wholesalers
ACME are manufacturers
Bosfit are manufacturers
BGM are manufacturers

Suppose that it is required to find out *whether Smiths is a retailer and a wholesaler*. Using the conjunction , it is possible to query as follows:

```
?-   retailer(smiths),wholesaler(smiths).
no
```

Suppose it is required to find out *who is a manufacturer and also a wholesaler*. Again the conjunction , is used:

```
?-   manufacturer(Who),wholesaler(Who).
Who = bgm;
```

If ; is now entered, Prolog responds with:

```
no
```

This is because it is unable to find any alternative solutions.

Another query might be to find out *whether BHS is either a manufacturer, a wholesaler or both*. In this case the disjunction ; is used:

```
?- manufacturer(bhs);wholesaler(bhs).
yes
```

To find out *who either retails or wholesales or both*, again the disjunction is used:

```
?- retailer(Who);wholesaler(Who).
Who = smiths;
Who = bhs;
Who = bgm;
Who = direct;
no
```

Using the negation, not, for the same database, query:

```
?- not(retailer(smiths)).
no
```

This means that the goal *Smiths is not a retailer* has failed. It might be inferred as true that *Smiths is a retailer* and this would, as a fact of the database, be correct.

Now try:

```
?- not(retailer(owens)).
yes
```

This says that the goal that *Owens is not a retailer* has succeeded; that *Owens is a retailer* is not asserted in the database.

Consider the query:

```
?- retailer(woolworths).
no
```

Prolog responds with no simply because it is not asserted in the database that *Woolworths is a retailer*. It does not respond with *don't know*.

Importantly, however, the query:

```
?- not(retailer(woolworths)).
yes
```

succeeds, since the previous goal is negated.

Now query:

```
?- retailer(not(smiths)).
no
```

This fails because the argument of the retailer predicate not(smiths) is not matched in the database. The interpretation that *there is a retailer that is not smiths* is not considered by Prolog,

Consider the query:

```
?- retailer(Who).
Who = smiths;
Who = bhs;
no
```

These responses would be expected from the database. But try:

```
?- not(retailer(Who)).
no
```

Try:

```
?- not(not(retailer(Who))).
yes
```

This query succeeds, since it is the negation of the previous goal, and that failed.

Note that spaces around logical connectives are ignored by Prolog. Thus:

```
retailer(Who)  ; wholesaler(Who).
```

and

```
retailer(Who);wholesaler(Who).
```

are processed in the same way.

Logical Connectives Exercise

Assert:

```
married(alan,marianne).
bore(marianne, jonathon).
loves(alan, marianne).
loves(marianne, alan).
loves(alan, jonathon).
loves(marianne, jonathon).
```

Here *Alan married Marianne, Marianne bore Jonathon* and *Alan loves Marianne* and so on are the interpretations. Now make the following queries and interpret the responses:

1. Alan married Marianne and Marianne bore Jonathon?
2. Marianne bore Jonathon and Alan married Marianne?
3. Alan loves Marianne and Marianne loves Alan?
4. Alan loves Marianne and Marianne loves Jonathon?
5. Alan loves Jonathon and Jonathon loves Alan?
6. Either Alan loves Marianne or Marianne loves Alan?
7. Either Alan loves Jonathon or Jonathon loves Alan?
8. Alan did not marry anyone?

9. Alan did not marry Marianne?
10. It is not the case that Marianne married Jonathon and that
    Jonathon loves Marianne?
11. Who does neither Marianne nor Jonathon love?

4.9 Rules

It was said earlier that clauses could contain conditional statements. For
Prolog to have the ability to arrive at conclusions, it is possible to use
conditional clauses or *rules*. Such clauses consist of the conclusion to be
arrived at, followed by : - and ending with the conditions which might lead
to that conclusion. When written in this way, the condition is referred to as
the *body* of the rule, and the conclusion is its *head*. Thus, *if it was sunny on
Thursday, it will be sunny on Friday* might be written as:

```
sunny(friday) :- sunny(thursday).
```

Here sunny(friday) is the *head* of the clause, and sunny(thursday)
is its *body*. Using the variable Anyday, the expression can be generalised to:

```
sunny(friday) :- sunny(Anyday).
```

(Note: Most versions of Prolog will display WARNING: Anyday used
only once or similar. This is a *style* correction facility. By responding to
a word which has only been used once, the user is warned of a possible mis-
spelling. Ignore this warning here and in most of the *short* examples and
exercises in this book.)

It will now be interpreted as *if it is sunny on any day, then it will be sunny
on Friday*. Remember that Anyday did not have to be used. Any word
beginning with a capital letter or an underscore, would have been just as
suitable.

When *general statements are to be made, quantification is understood.*
Conversely there is no need to be concerned about the instantiation process.
The important point to remember is that *quantification is restricted to
individual clauses*.

Thus *He is a gardener and He is a handyman*, could be entered as:

```
gardener(He), handyman(He).
```

However, consider the following:

```
gardener(He). handyman(He).
```

This would be *he was a gardener, and he (the same person or another) is a
handyman* because He is redefined.

Often in order to make a program run, a keyword is used as the head of a
rule, the keyword being a predicate with no argument. The body of this rule
is the rest of the program. For example:

```
run_program:- Program
?- run_program.
```

This causes `Program` to be executed.

Rules Examples

These examples are not intended to be run, but to illustrate the way in which rules are written in Prolog.

1. All computer scientists are clever.
    (If Someone is a computer scientist then Someone is clever.)

    ```
    clever(Someone) :-
        computer_scientist(Someone).
    ```

2. These are examples of the ways in which you can start to define a family tree.

    ```
    family(Male, Female) :-
        husband(Male),wife(Female).
    family(Male, Female, Child) :-
        husband(Male), wife(Female),
        (child(Male, Child),
        child(Female, Child)).
    ```

Rules Exercise

Express these rules in Prolog syntax.

1. A goldfish is a pet.
2. All apples are edible.
3. A schoolchild is young, human and goes to school.
4. If you take, you should give as well.

4.10 Empty Heads

The `:-` symbol which is usually associated with a rule, is often used to specify what are called *directives*. These are rules which have a body, but no head.

One use includes interaction with the user. Thus:

```
:- write(enter your choice now).
```

will cause the words `enter your choice now` to appear on the screen. The `write` predicate will be returned to in chapter seven. Empty heads are also used with the op predicate, described in the *Operators* section.

4.11 Making Queries

We have already seen that once a database has been entered into Prolog the user will want to query it, often by asking whether a certain fact is true. Prolog will answer yes if the queried fact matches with a fact in its database. no will be the reply if there is no such match.

When a query is entered, it constitutes a *goal* for the program. The goal succeeds if the response is yes. A *simple query*, has a *single* goal.

The predicate call(Goal) has the same effect as asking the query:

```
?- Goal
```

It can be used within a program, to find the response to a goal, instead of using the query prompt. For example:
Assert:

```
callex:-
call(father(chris,martin)).
father(chris,martin).
?- callex.
yes
```

Note that the clause to be called must appear after the call predicate in the program. If not the search will fail:

```
callex_a:-
father(chris,martin).
call(father(chris,martin)).
?- callex_a.
no
```

Here is a further example:

```
callex_b:-
call(father(chris,chris)).
father(chris,martin).
?- callex_b.
no
```

Query Examples

Assert the following:

```
reptile(lizard).
reptile(tortoise).
fish(minnow).
mammal(whale).
bird(hawk).
```

Now query:

```
?- reptile(lizard).
yes
?- lizard(reptile).
WARNING: no clause for relation lizard/1
no
```

This warning is issued because a predicate for lizard has not yet been defined.

```
?- fish(dolphin).
   no
?- fish(perch).
   no
```

Even though perch is a fish, the correct answer will not be given, because perch has not been defined in Prolog's database.

An *existential query* is one in which the goal succeeds if instantiations of variables are sought from the database and named, rather than there being a simple *yes/no* response. If there are no satisfactory instantiations, the goal fails and the response is no. If further solutions are sought, the semicolon ; is entered after each response until the response is no. This indicates that there are no further instantiations available from the database.

Further Query Examples

Using the database for the previous Query examples:

```
?- reptile(X).
X = lizard;
X = tortoise;
no
?- reptile(x).
no
```

(A lower case x is treated as a constant, and not a variable.)

```
?- reptile(Lizard).
Lizard = lizard;
Lizard = tortoise;
no
```

(Because Lizard starts with a capital letter, Prolog considers it to be a variable)

Now assert:

```
father(chris, david).
```

```
father(chris, martin).
father(sidney, chris).
father(sidney, diane).
```

Query:

```
?- father(chris, martin).
yes
?- father(chris, Offspring).
Offspring = david;
Offspring = martin;
no
?- father(Father, Offspring).
Father = chris
Offspring = david;
Father = chris
Offspring = martin;
Father = sidney
Offspring = chris;
Father = sidney
Offspring = diane;
no
```

Queries Exercise

1. Assert the following:

```
footballer(john).
footballer(james).
swimmer(harold).
golfer(john).
```

Predict how Prolog will respond for the following queries:

```
a) ?- footballer(john).
b) ?- footballer(X).
c) ?- footballer(chris).
d) ?- footballer(John).
```

2. Assert:

```
aunt(mabel, diane).
aunt(mabel, joanne).
aunt(diane, john).
aunt(diane, eve).
aunt(joanne, mabel).
```

Predict the answer which would be given to the following queries.

```
a)      ?- aunt(mabel, joanne).
b)      ?- aunt(mabel, Niece).
c)      ?- aunt(Aunt, Niece).
```

4.12 Built-in Predicates

A programmer will design and use predicates, in respect of the real life situation which is being modelled. There are also built-in predicates which are part of the Prolog software. These vary with the version of Prolog being used.

Some of the built-in predicates are of direct value in the modelling process. Others, sometimes called *extralogical*, are not: Search control predicates control the mechanics of the proof process. System predicates allow Prolog to interface with the computer system being used. Text predicates allow text to be presented in the most legible way.

Examples of system predicates are `op`, `write`, `consult` and `reconsult`.

4.13 Operators

When more than one predicate or operator is present in a clause, the order in which the relations are considered will generally make a difference to the value arrived at. Using an arithmetic example, `16/2+6` might produce the answers `14` or `2`, depending on whether or not the division precedes the addition. The convention is that division precedes addition in this case.

When an operator is defined in Prolog, a precedence number must be attached to it. This determines the order in which it is to be performed relative to other operators. This is known as its *operator precedence number*, and ranges from *1* to about *1500*. A *lower* precedence number implies a *stronger* bonding. The precedence numbers for the most commonly occurring built-in operators, are included in the appendices to this book.

Brackets can alternatively be used to specify precedence. This may result in an unwieldy and clumsy formulation in some cases, however.

The *associativity* of an operator governs the way in which pairs of elements in an expression, are to be combined with each other. For instance, *(a # b) # c* may not have the same value as *a # (b # c)*. Associativity of an operator is determined by its *type*, whether *infix*, *postfix* or *prefix*. An operator is *non-associative*, when the order in which the operations are carried out, does not affect the outcome. In Prolog, this is achieved by giving the component expression a lower precedence than the original one.

A *left-associative* operator is such that it has a left hand argument which is of the same precedence or lower than the original operator. A *right-associative* operator is such that its right hand argument is of the same precedence or lower than the original one. The built-in operator + for arithmetic addition is left associative, as is that for subtraction -. Accordingly: 8 - 7 + 4 is represented, using postfix notation and brackets to convey associativity: +(-(8,7),4). There is a built-in predicate display which actually displays an expression in this way, making the associativity self-evident.

4.14 Declaring an operator

To declare an operator, the built-in predicate op is used. This is of the form:

op(Precedence, Type, Name)

Here, Precedence is the desired operator precedence. Type is the type of operator, whether infix, postfix or prefix. This will determine the associativity. Name is the name given to that particular operator.

Operators Examples

Operators are declared using *headless clauses*. For example:

:- op(300, xfy, &)

defines the infix operator & with precedence 300.

:- op(600, fx, [-, +]).

defines the postfix operator [-, +] with precedence 600.

The following table gives the associativities of the different types of operators:

fx	*non-associative*	*prefix*
fy	*right-associative*	*prefix*
xf	*non-associative*	*postfix*
yf	*left-associative*	*postfix*
xfx	*non-associative*	*infix*
xfy	*right-associative*	*infix*
yfx	*left-associative*	*infix*

Here are some examples of the way in which the type of an operator # affects its associativity:

type *yfx (left associative)*:
    P # Q # R # S = #(#(#(P, Q), R), D)
type *xfy (right associative)*:
    P # Q # R# S = #(P, #(Q, #(R, S)))

Operators Exercise

1.Define the operators @ and $ to behave as infix operators in the following formats:

   a)   *@(@(@(X,Y),Z),W),*
   b)   *$(X,$(Y,$(Z,W)))$(X,@(Y,Z)).*

2. Using the list of operator precedences in Appendix 5, predict Prolog's response to each of the following:

   a)   `?- display(x > y * z),`
   b)   `?- display(x mod y div z),`
   c)   `?- display(x is y - z),`
   d)   `?- display(x * y =:= z).`

4.15 Blank Variables

There are occasions when, although it is known that a variable is present in a relation, it is neither necessary, possible nor desirable to give instantiations of it. In this situation, the *blank* or *anonymous* variable is used, symbolised by an underscore.

Blank Variables Examples

For example, the rule that *a wife must be married*, is written:

```
married(She) :- wife(She, _).
```

Literally, *if she is the wife of anyone then she is married.* It is not necessary to know exactly whom She is married to.
Assert:

```
wife(marianne,_).
```

Query:

```
?- married(marianne).
yes
```

Assert:

```
wife(Spouse) :- married(Spouse, _).
married(janet, chris).
married(caren, gerald).
child(janet, chris, martin).
child(caren, gerald, deborah).
boy(martin).
girl(deborah).
son(Son) :- child(_, _, Son), boy(Son).
daughter(Daughter) :- child(_, _, Daughter),
```

```
        girl(Daughter).
```
Query:

```
        ?- wife(Who).
        Who = janet;
        Who = caren;
        no
```
Query:

```
        ?- child(_, _, Who).
        Who = martin;
        Who = deborah;
        no
```
Query:

```
        ?- married(_, Who).
        Who = chris;
        Who = gerald;
        no
```
Query:

```
        ?- married(_, _).
        yes
```

Blank Variable Exercise

Utilise the blank variable to define the rule that a friend is someone who is liked by another person.

4.16 Equality

Prolog has a number of built-in predicates for testing and asserting equality. The = predicate succeeds if two variables will match. The \= conversely succeeds when = fails and vice versa. When = succeeds, it does so by instantiation to particular values. If one of the variables is uninstantiated, it will receive the value of the other instantiated variable. For example:
Query:

```
        ?-  This = That.
        This = _1
        That = _1
        yes
```

Query:

```
        ?-  This = This.
```

```
This = _1
yes
```

There is a similar, but stricter, form of equality, ==, which will only consider an uninstantiated variable equal to another uninstantiated variable. Numerical forms of equality are discussed in chapter six .

4.17 Recursion

A *recursive* process is one which repeats according to some rule. Thus, if a case of floppy discs has to be emptied for cleaning, the discs could be taken out one at a time and rested on the table. The process of removing a disc and placing it on the table is applied to the stock of discs in the case. Ultimately, the case will be emptied and the process halted. There is a similarity to what happens, when a loop and a decision command are used, in some other computer languages.

A rule can be defined recursively in Prolog, by relating a present value of a term, by a rule, to a previous value. For example, the *nth* natural number can be obtained from the *(n-1)th* natural number by adding one, and this will work for all natural numbers. A Prolog recursive rule will always need a boundary condition at which to terminate. This may seem odd at first, but it is due to the search strategy used by Prolog which is carried out *backwards*. Thus, to make this recursive process terminate, the value *1* is presented as the terminal result of repeatedly *subtracting* one to get the *preceding* natural number.

Recursion Examples

A recursive rule is one in which the current value of a term is defined in terms of a previous one. Consider the relation parent_of(X,Y) meaning *X is the parent of Y*. The following facts are given:

```
parent_of(evan, adrian).
parent_of(adrian, james).
parent_of(james, alan).
```

Now, suppose it is wished to describe the ancestry of alan. Recursion can be used to advantage here. A predicate ancestor_of(X,Y) meaning X is an ancestor of Y can be defined. When only a single generation is required, this will be the same as the parent_of relation which gives the rule:

```
ancestor_of(Older,Younger):-
    parent_of(Older,Younger).
```

This implies that if someone is the parent of someone else, then they are an ancestor of them. It gives a boundary condition for recursion. The recursion is made to work over successive generations using the rule:

```
ancestor_of(Older,Younger):-
   parent_of(Older,In_between),
   ancestor_of(In_between,Younger).
```

This adds that if someone is the parent of another, and that person is the ancestor of a third person, then the first person is an ancestor of the last. Using this rule it is possible to cover as many generations as is required, since it is always possible to get from one generation to the next.
Query:

```
?- ancestor_of(evan,james).
yes
```

Query:

```
?-  ancestor_of(Who,james).
Who = adrian;
Who = evan;
no
```

The boundary condition provides a stopping point for the search. Interestingly, if the conjunctions in the body of the second rule are reversed, the program will still give the correct responses, but will terminate after the last ; and an error statement: out of stack space, or equivalent will appear. This procedural difference is because the variable Younger is uninstantiated at the point that the recursive subgoal ancestor_of(In_between,Younger) is evaluated. Accordingly, although the correct solutions for the goal are found, the search continues in a recursive loop until no memory is remaining to store details of that loop.

The next example concerns a network of manufacturers, wholesalers, retailers and agents, all of whom handle some commodity. There is a relation supplies which may hold between a manufacturer and a wholesaler, between a wholesaler and a retailer, and also between a retailer and an agent:

```
supplies(bgm,direct).
supplies(direct,bhs).
supplies(bhs,'Harding, L.').
```

The predicate supplier will now be introduced. A source of a commodity is a relation which can be transitive (ie. passed on). supplier is intended to capture this relation.

```
supplier(Initial,Final):-
   supplies(Initial,Final).
supplier(Initial,Final):-
   supplies(Initial,Intermediary),
```

```
        supplier(Intermediary,Final).
```

These queries can be made:

```
        ?- supplies(Who, 'Harding, L.').
        % Who supplies Harding, L ?
        Who = bhs ;
        no
```

This query only makes use of direct supplies from a retailer to an agent. If the agent is desperate for supplies, it might be necessary to look further back than a retailer. This will happen if the supplier predicate is used:

```
        ?- supplier(Who, 'Harding, L.')
        % Who is a supplier ?
        Who = bhs ;
        Who = bgm ;
        Who = direct ;
        no
```

Recursion Exercise

1. Apply the ancestor predicate to your own ancestry.
2. Define recursive rules using a predicate route_to, which defines the routes possible between any two stations of a railway network. Test the program using a local rail map.

4.18 Updating a Running Program

It is possible to update a running program from the query prompt. There are two main built-in predicates for this purpose, assert(Clause) and retract(Clause). However, the way in which these are used varies from version to version. If in doubt, it will be necessary to refer to the relevant Prolog System Manual.

In any event, the original intention for Prolog was as follows: If a new clause is to be added to a program, the predicate assert(Clause) is used. The built in predicate asserta(Clause) will add Clause to the beginning of the list of those already defined. To add a clause to the end, the predicate assertz(Clause) is used.

Conversely, a clause may need to be removed. retract(Clause) removes instances of Clause one at a time. Thus,

```
        ?- assertz((parent(Older,Younger):-
           father(Older,Younger)).
```

will cause the clause,

```
?- parent(Older,Younger):-
   father(Older,Younger).
```
to be added to the end of Prolog's database, while,
```
?- retract((parent(Older,Younger):-
   father(Older,Younger))).
```

will cause the first occurrence of that clause to be removed. Further occurrences will require further retractions. Notice the double brackets which are used with the retract predicate.

Updating Examples

Consider the program:
```
friends(david, richard).
friends(david, jonathon).
friends(richard, alan).
```
Now query,
```
?- friends(david, matthew).
no
```
Enter,
```
?- assert(friends(david, matthew)).
```
Query,
```
?- friends(david, matthew).
yes
```
Enter,
```
?- retract((friends(david, matthew))).
```
Query,
```
?- friends(david, matthew).
no
```
Enter,
```
?- retract((friends(david, Who))).
```
Then query,
```
?- friends(david,richard).
no
?- friends(david,Who).
Who = jonathon ;
no
```

The last few queries illustrate that only the first occurrence of a clause is being retracted on each occasion. However, be careful, since entering ; after each response will, step by step, remove all occurrences of the clause.

Updating Exercise

Assert:

```
retailer(smiths).
retailer(bhs).
wholesaler(bgm).
wholesaler(direct).
manufacturer(acme).
manufacturer(bosfit).
manufacturer(bgm).
```

Work out Prolog's response before making the following queries:
Query:

```
?- retailer(Who).
```

Enter:

```
?- retract(retailer(smiths)).
```

Query:

```
?- retailer(Who).
```

Enter:

```
?- retract(wholesaler(Who)).
```

Query:

```
?- wholesaler(Who).
```

Enter:

```
?- retract(wholesaler(Who)).
```

Query:

```
?- wholesaler(Who).
```

Enter:

```
?- assert(wholesaler(bgm)).
```

Query:

```
?- wholesaler(Who).
```

Enter:

```
?- assert(wholesaler(bgm)).
```

Query:

```
?- wholesaler(Who).
```

4.19 Lists

The data for a Prolog program frequently appears as a list of items. Because this data structure occurs so often, there is a special predicate called *list*, and there are many useful operations that can be carried out upon lists with its use. This predicate is dealt with fully in chapter *8*, on data structures, where it can be considered alongside the other ways in which data can be represented in Prolog. However, since it is impossible to completely avoid the use of lists, even at an early stage of learning Prolog, a few introductory words are given here.

Essentially, a list such as:

> *alan, bernice, charles*

can be written in Prolog as

```
[alan, bernice, charles]
```

It can be named as a list:

```
L = [alan, bernice, charles].
```

Operations may then be carried out on L. For instance, the first member of the list may be extracted from the remainder, a particular member may be displayed, or the order of the list varied in a variety of ways.

4.20 Applications

DEDUCTIVE INFORMATION RETRIEVAL SYSTEM

The following short program enables deductions to be made from a given database. The database is:

> *John likes Mary.*
> *John likes Jane.*
> *Mary likes Pete.*
> *Pete likes Kate.*
> *Jane likes John.*
> *Kate likes everyone.*

The program is included with thanks to Warren (1975).

```
% DEDUCTIVE INFORMATION RETRIEVAL.

% LOGIC PROGRAM
:-   op(900, xfy, &).
:-   op(700, xfy, likes).

% DATA
john likes mary.
john likes jane.
```

```
mary likes pete.
pete likes kate.
jane likes john.
kate likes _.
```

The following can be considered: *Who likes someone, and is liked back?*

```
?- X likes Y, Y likes X, write((X & Y)).
john & jane;
pete & kate;
jane & john;
kate & pete;
kate & kate;
no
```

SYMPTOMOLOGY

In the diagnosis of disease, a number of symptoms are often considered through a process of careful examination by a physician. There then follows a logical puzzle, where different combinations of symptoms may point to different diseases. In reality, this process is complicated by the fact that there is no certainty that a given disease will give rise to particular symptoms in a given patient.

The present application is not particularly refined, and deals with an all-or-nothing idealisation, in which the occurrence or non-occurrence of specific symptoms points unequivocally to specific diseases. The program could be used to check a diagnosis. No natural diseases are named because of the shortcomings, but instead we start with the information:

Disease A has symptoms P, R, and S.
Disease B has symptom P only.
Disease C has symptoms P, Q, R, S.
Disease D has symptoms R and S.

```
% SYMPTOMOLOGY
diagnosis(a_disease, p_symptom,
  q_symptom_absent,r_symptom, s_symptom).
diagnosis(b_disease,p_symptom,
  q_symptom_absent,
  r_symptom_absent, s_symptom_absent).
diagnosis(c_disease, p_symptom, q_symptom,
  r_symptom,s_symptom).
diagnosis(d_disease, p_symptom_absent,
  q_symptom_absent,r_symptom, s_symptom).
?-diagnosis(b_disease,p_symptom,
```

```
        q_symptom_absent,r_symptom_absent,
        s-symptom_absent).
yes
?-      diagnosis(b_disease, p_symptom,
        q_symptom, r_symptom,      s_symptom).
no
```

The form of the above program can be used as a starting point for a teaching program where a set of related facts has to be learned. For instance, still in the medical domain, an anatomy tutor might use the predicate,

```
fact(Muscle, Origin, Insertion, Innervation).
```

and use the following as a data base:

```
fact(pronator_teres, humerus_and_ulna,
    radius,median).
fact(flexor_carpi_radialis, humerus,
    metacarpals, median).
fact(flexor_carpi_ulnaris, humerus_and_ulna,
    metacarpals,  ulnar).
```

A query will only succeed if the user gives the correct combination of muscle, origin, insertion and innervation.

Chapter Five
GOAL SEARCHING AND
ITS CONTROL

5.1 Goals

When answering a query and searching for a goal, Prolog looks for a *match* where the predicates and their arguments are the same as in the query. This match can be from the database, or any intermediate places along the search path. Put another way, attempts are made to find a clause in the database from which the goal *follows*. If there is a successful match, Prolog will respond with yes. Alternatively if terms are not identical, variables may be instantiated. An integer or atom will match only itself. A more complicated structure will match another structure with the same relation and arity, provided that all corresponding arguments match.

The = connective introduced in the previous chapter, effectively matches two formulae, and may be used by a programmer to achieve a deliberate match in a search.

Goals Examples

Consider the following database:

```
retailer(smiths).
retailer(bhs).    .
wholesaler(bgm).
wholesaler(direct).
manufacturer(acme).
manufacturer(bosfit).
manufacturer(bgm).
```

Query:

```
?- retailer(smiths).
yes
```

Prolog searches the database until it finds a match, first for the predicate retailer and then for the constant smiths. It succeeds at the top of the

database and answers yes.
Query:

```
?- retailer(bosfit).
no
```

Prolog searches the database from the top as before. It matches the predicate
`retailer`, but cannot match the argument bhs as well. It therefore
responds with no.
Query:

```
?- retailer(Who).
Who = smiths ;
Who = bhs ;
no
```

First Prolog matches the predicate `retailer`, it then instantiates the
variable Who to smiths, displays the information and waits. If ; is entered
it searches for a further instantiation and finds bhs. If the semi-colon is
entered again, Prolog searches in vain for a further instantiation for Who in
`retailer`. As a result, no is displayed.

The search process is not random. It filters from *top to bottom*, in the order
that clauses are presented in the database. Rules are resolved from *left to
right*. If Prolog is unsuccessful having searched down a branch of its *search
tree*, it will have to *backtrack*. This also happens if instructed to look for
further solutions. Backtracking involves the search returning to the original
goal, or to a previous point of the search, in order to find an alternative route
to the goal.

Consider the following program, which helps to show how the search
process works. It concerns a marketing network of manufacturers,
wholesalers and retailers, in which a predicate called `supplies` is defined.
Using this program, it can be ascertained who supplies whom.

```
retailer(smiths).
retailer(bhs).
wholesaler(bgm).
wholesaler(direct).
manufacturer(acme).
manufacturer(bosfit).
supplies(Outward, Inward):-
    manufacturer(Outward),
    wholesaler(Inward).
supplies(Outward, Inward):-
    wholesaler(Outward), retailer(Inward).
```

The goal,

```
?- retailer(smiths).% Are Smith's retailers?
```

would be reached as follows: At the top of the database, the predicate `retailer` is matched. The argument `smiths` is also matched, so that the goal is satisfied and `yes` is the response.

Now consider the query:

```
?- retailer(Who).% Who are retailers?
```

At the top of the database, `retailer` is matched. The variable `Who` can also be matched to `smiths`. Therefore,

```
Who = smiths
```

appears on the computer screen. This is Prolog answering that `smiths` is a retailer. The search will rest at this point, until `;` is entered by the user. Then `bhs` will be found and,

```
Who = bhs
```

will be the response. Further entry of `;` does not result in any more matching, and as a consequence, `no` is answered.

A more complicated query is

```
?- supplies(bgm, Who).% Who does bgm supply?
```

Searching from the top as usual, there is nothing that matches `supplies` except the head of the rule,

```
supplies(Outward, Inward):-
    manufacturer(Outward),
    wholesaler(Inward).
```

Here the variable `Outward` is represented as bgm, since moving to the right of the rule, `manufacturer(Outward)` can be instantiated to `manufacturer(bgm)`. However, `manufacturer(bgm)` was not asserted, and so the rule is abandoned without looking at the `wholesaler` data. The search then moves down to the next `supplies` rule:

```
supplies(Outward, Inward):-
    wholesaler(Outward), retailer(Inward).
```

`wholesaler(Outward)` is instantiated to `wholesaler(bgm)` which succeeds, since it is an assertion of the database. The search then moves to `retailer(Inward)` matching `retailer` to `retailer(smiths)`.

Thus,

```
Who = smiths
```

is output to the user, and subsequently, after entering a `;` so is:

```
Who = bhs
```

Enter

     ;

The response is:

     `no`

The query,

     `?- supplies(Who, Whom)% Who supplies Whom?`

requires a much longer search, and so a search tree has been constructed for reference, in Fig. 5.1. The predicate `supplies` is the first to be found, in the rule:

     `supplies(Outward, Inward):-`
         `manufacturer(Outward),wholesaler(Inward).`

The subgoals `manufacturer(Outward)` and `wholesaler(Inward)` are instantiated to acme and bgm respectively. Thus,

     `Outward = acme`
     `Inward = bgm`

is the response. Entering *;* causes backtracking to find another instantiation of `wholesaler(Inward)`, namely `direct`. As a result,

     `Outward = acme`
     `Inward = direct`

is presented to the user. Using *;* to search for a further instantiation of `wholesaler(Inward)` fails, and so the previous subgoal `manufacturer(Outward)` is backtracked to. This is instantiated to `bosfit`. The search then proceeds to again find instantiations for `wholesaler(Inward)`. bgm is found, with the following output:

     `Outward = bosfit`
     `Inward = bgm`

Further use of *;* finds that,

     `Outward = bosfit`
     `Inward = direct`

Although all of the possibilities for the first rules are now exhausted, the search will move back to the second rule,

     `supplies(Outward,Inward):-`
         `wholesaler(Outward),retailer(Inward)`

and finally to the rule,

     `supplies(Outward,Inward):-`
         `manufacturer(Outward),retailer(Inward).`

When the search is complete, use of ; will give the no response since no further matching is possible.

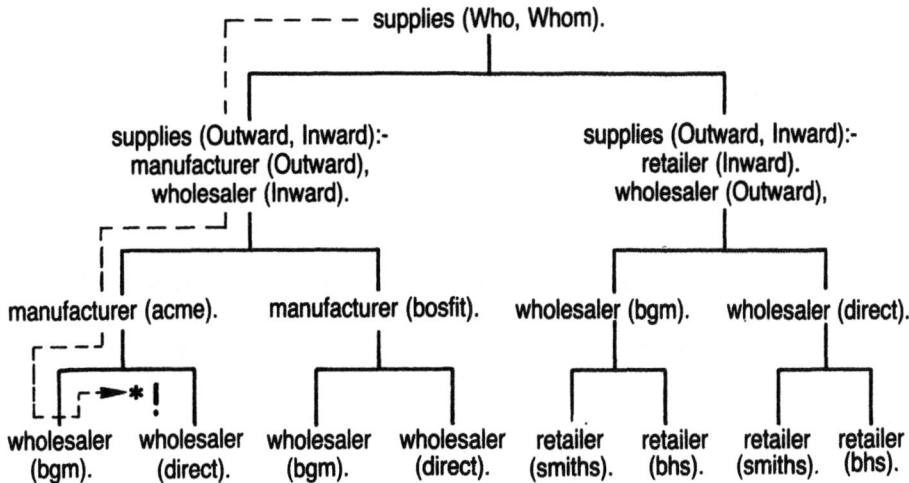

Figure 5.1

Goals Exercise

The following program contains the conditions for someone to be promoted in a company. To be promoted, it is necessary to be a staff member of the department concerned. They must also have been proposed by the present head of their department, as well as being properly qualified.

```
staff(moss, accounts).
staff(james, accounts).
staff(philips, library).
staff(owens, accounts).
proposed(james, accounts).
proposed(philips, library).
proposed(owens, accounts).
qualified(philips).
qualified(james).
promotion(Name, Dept):-
     staff(Name, Dept), proposed(Name, Dept),
     qualified(Name).
```

1) Find out who can be promoted from the library.
2) Draw search trees for the following queries:

```
?- promotion(Who, accounts).
Who = james;
no
?- promotion(Who, Where).
Who = james
Where = accounts;
Who = philips
Where = library;
no
```

5.2 Search Control

The amount of time spent searching and backtracking to achieve a match can be greatly reduced, if the programmer eliminates search paths, known at the outset to not lead to a solution. There are built in predicates to assist here. The *cut* ! predicate prevents the search from backtracking. It can be compared to a *one-way valve*. From a programmer's point of view, it enables specific goals to determine the stopping point of a search.

Because of Prolog's search technique, ! acts on all clauses below it in the search tree. It effectively eliminates alternative solutions to goals appearing to its left in a clause. However, goals to the right of ! are not affected.

It is sometimes desirable to use the not predicate instead of !, since the resulting program is easier to read.

Going back to Figure 5.1, it might be required to find only a single supplier of the goods in question, before aborting the search. The clause,

```
find_supplier(Who,Whom):-
    supplies(Who,Whom), !.
```

uses ! to stop the search after a supplier has been found.

Here are two queries, using the amended clause:

```
?-   find_supplier(acme,Whom).
%    Find somebody supplied by acme.
Whom = bgm;
no
?-   find_supplier(Who,bgm).
%    Find somebody who supplies bgm.
```

Referring to Figure 5.1, once the search has passed *, (the first instantiation of Wholesaler to bgm) the presence of cut prevents backtracking to manufacturer(acme) and thence to further solutions. The search tree is clearly a useful tool for deciding where to place not or ! in a program.

Search Control Exercise

Refer to your answer for the Goals Exercise. How would you modify the program so that only one candidate is presented for promotion, regardless of the department ?

5.3 Extra Search Control Predicates

We now consider some further search control predicates. If fail is found in a search, the search is terminated as unsuccessful.

If true is encountered, the goal is successful, and further solutions may be sought. However, this predicate is not usually necessary if clauses or rules are properly structured.

The predicate not(Goal) succeeds if Goal fails, and fails if not(Goal) succeeds. It may by now be anticipated that not(not(Goal)) is not equivalent to Goal, since when a goal fails, its variables are uninstantiated.

The predicate repeat generates a never-ending number of backtracking choices, non-deterministically.

Extra Search Control Predicates Examples

By using fail, a program can be made to backtrack even if a goal has been successful. It is generally used together with ! in such situations. As an example, the following program reads a sentence to find a given word, disqualified.

```
find_word(Sentence) :-
read(Word,!,found(Word,Sentence),check(Word).
check(disqualified):-
    write('word''disqualified''found').
check(_):- fail.
found(Word,[Word|_]).
found(Word,[_|Tail]):- found(Word,Tail).
```

The program is used as follows:

```
?-   find_word(Sentence).
%    Type in sentence as a list
[mcquerty,is,disqualified,for, two,years].
word 'disqualified' found
Sentence =
[mcquerty,is,disqualified,for,two,years]
```

In this program, fail is used to make sure that after the word sought is found and checked as a successful goal, the program proceeds to the next word. The cut in the first rule is required to prevent the entire sentence being re-read in the case the required word is not actually present.

When the `repeat` predicate is found in a search, the search continues as if no backtracking had occurred. Subsequently more solutions are presented.

For example:

Assert:

```
manufacturer(acme).
manufacturer(bosfit).
manufacturer(bgm).
many(Who):- repeat, manufacturer(Who).
once(Who):- manufacturer(Who).
```

Query:

```
?- once(Who).
Who = acme ;
Who = bosfit ;
Who = bgm ;
no
```

As expected, all instantiations for the `manufacturer` predicate are given.
Query:

```
?- many(Who).
Who = acme ;
Who = bosfit ;
Who = bgm ;
Who = acme ;
Who = bosfit ;
Who = bgm ;
. . . . . . . . . . . .
```

This time, the program does not terminate. When the `manufacturer` instantiations are all covered once, the `repeat` predicate causes the search to re-commence. This process continues indefinitely.

Extra Search Predicates Exercise

1. Draw a search tree for the previous example and investigate the operation of the `repeat` command.

2. Use the `fail` predicate to express the sentence:

The Schoolboy lost all of his books except for Mathematics.

Chapter Six
ARITHMETIC AND MATHEMATICS

6.1 Introduction

At its inception, Prolog was not intended to be a language for arithmetic calculation and early versions were distinctly ill-equipped in this respect. There was a restriction to positive integer arithmetic. There was an absence of the kind of mathematical functions essential to the applied sciences such as the *trigonometric*, *exponential* and *logarithmic* functions. Nonetheless Prolog has always had the potential to define predicates for evaluating such functions.

Similarly, although there were no built-in operations of *differentiation* and *integration*, defining programs for these operations presented no insurmountable difficulties, even if some ingenuity was required.

The arithmetic capabilities of Prolog now extend to real number arithmetic instead of just integer arithmetic. This has dramatically widened the range of practical applications to which Prolog may be applied.

Prolog may also use *floating point* numbers, which may or may not make use of exponential notation. Floating point numbers are those containing a decimal point. They must contain at least one digit before the point, and one after, even if these digits have to be zero. The following are examples of floating point numbers:

$$2.0 \qquad 346.713 \qquad -13.2$$

The exponential form used by Prolog is essentially *standard form*. Instead of writing *165000000* it is possible to write *1.6e8* or *1.6E8*. Here, the number before the *E* or *e* is multiplied by *10* to the power of the number after it. Similarly, *0.000016*, can be written as *1.6E-5*. It is vital not to include spaces within such numbers.

Alongside these improvements in arithmetic, libraries of mathematical functions have been included which Prolog can access. Prolog can make use of all of the most widely used mathematical functions, as standard built-in predicates. Also included are predicates which can generate pseudo random numbers.

Some of the examples in this chapter will, in view of what has just been said, seem of little practical value. However, they should not be skipped. For one thing they provide experience of the basic arithmetic predicates of Prolog, and applications of them. For another, not all mathematical functions may be available on a given version of Prolog, and so the programmer may well have to define his or her own.

6.2 Arithmetic Predicates

In the following, I and J are integers, Prolog offers the following arithmetic operators:

I + J	the numerical sum of I and J.
I - J	the numerical difference between I and J.
I * J	the product of I and J.
I // J	the integer division of I by J. (any remainder is ignored).
I / J	real number division of I by J. (A decimal answer is given).
I mod J	the remainder when I is divided by J.
I ^ J	I raised to the power J.

When the answer to a calculation is required, the predicate is is used, and not the equals = symbol. Thus X is 1+2 will cause Prolog to return X = 3. The introduction of is in this way is not without reason. The = predicate has been introduced previously. It will succeed when the two entities being compared match, or instantiate to values which will match. Because of this, an arithmetic equation such as 2 + 1 = 3 will fail, even though it is arithmetically correct. Ironically, 2 + 3 \= 5 will succeed, since the entities 2 + 3 and 5 do not match. The predicate is takes account of any arithmetic operations being used, before attempting to match the goal.

It is possible to compare numbers by using the following operators:

I =:= J	Succeeds if the instantiated values of I and J are the same. If only one of the variables is instantiated, then the other will take that value.
I =/= J	Succeeds if I and J are not instantiated to the same value.
I < J	Succeeds if I is less than J.
I > J	Succeeds if I is greater than J.
I >= J	Succeeds if I is greater than or equal to J.
I =< J	Succeeds if I is less than or equal to J. The order of the < and = signs must be as written.

Arithmetic Predicates Examples

Here are some examples, executed with Prolog in query mode.

User	Prolog
?- C is 3 + 5.	C = 8
?- A is 3, B is A + 1.	
	A = 3
	B = 4
?- Y is 4, X is Y - 1.	
	Y = 4
	X = 3
?- C is 2, D is C * 2.	
	C = 2
	D = 4
?- D is 8, C is D/2.	
	D = 8
	C = 4
?- D is 9, C is D/2.	
	D = 9
	C = 4.5
?- D is 9, C is D//2.	
	D = 9
	C = 4
?- C is (9 mod 2).	
	C = 1
?- A is 3, B is 10, C is 5, D is 6, E is ((A * B)/ C)+D.	
	A = 3
	B = 10
	C = 5
	D = 6
	E = 12

Arithmetic Predicates Exercise

Work out the responses that will be given to each of the following queries.

1.   ?- A is 4,
                B is 5,
                A > B.
2.   ?- C is 4 + 7.
3.   ?- A is 6.
                B is A + 4.
4.   ?- Y is 11,
                X is Y - 5.
5.   ?- C is 8,
                D is 4 * C.
6.   ?- D is 36,
                C is D/9.
7.   ?- D is 31,
                C is D/5.
8.   ?- C is (17 mod 5).
9.   ?- C is 17/3, D is (17 mod 3).
10.   ?- A is 3,
                B is 12,
                C is 5,
                D is 6,
                E is ((A + B)/ C)*D.
11.   ?- X is 5,
                Y is 3,
                Z is 8,
                A is X + Y,
                B is X * Z,
                C is B/A.

6.3 Programs using Arithmetic Predicates

The following program uses Prolog arithmetic. Given the electrical current used, it instructs the user on whether to use a one amp, two amp, five amp or ten amp fuse.

```
range(one_amp, 0, 1).
range(two_amp, 1, 2).
range(five_amp, 2, 5).
range(ten_amp, 5, 10).
use(A, B) :- range(A, X, Y),
B =< Y,
B >= X.
```

```
?- use(Fuse, 4).
Fuse = five_amp
```

This program can be extended so that only information on the power rating and voltage is required. It uses the fact that the current used is equal to the power consumed, divided by the supply voltage.

```
range(one_amp, 0, 1).
range(two_amp, 1, 2).
range(five_amp, 2, 5).
range(ten_amp, 5, 10).
rating(F, P, V):-range(F, X, Y),(P//V)=<Y,
    (P//V) >= X.
% For a 40 watt light running on 12
% volts:
?- rating(Fuse, 40, 12).
    Fuse = five_amp
```

The next program will convert a given number of seconds into days, hours, minutes and seconds.

```
change(Input,Days,Hours,Minutes,Seconds):-
Seconds is (Input mod 60),
Mintot is (Input//60),
Minutes is (Mintot mod 60),
Hourtot is (Mintot//60),
Hours is (Hourtot mod 24),
Daytot is (Hourtot // 24),
Days is (Daytot mod 24).
?- change(90061,Days,Hours,Minutes,Seconds).
    Days = 1
    Hours = 1
    Minutes = 1
    Seconds = 1
```

Arithmetic Programs Exercise

1. Adapt the last program so that it is able to change any whole number less than *127*, into any number base less than ten.

2. Design a program using a recursive definition, to find the *n*th triangle number. The triangle numbers are the sum of the positive integers up to and including the integer *n*.

3. Design a program to divide two integers, giving an answer expressed as a mixed number or vulgar fraction.

4. Design a program which divides two integers, giving a decimal answer to three decimal places.

5. Use a recursive definition to give the factorial of a positive integer. The

factorial of a positive integer is the product of all the positive integers up to and including itself. For example *5* factorial is *5 x 4 x 3 x 2 x 1 = 120*. It is written *5!*. *0!* is taken as *1*, and this should be taken as the boundary condition.

6.4 Mathematical Functions

The example below models a *quadratic* function. All quadratic functions are of the form:

$$f(x) = ax^2 + bx + c$$

Here, *a*, *b* and *c* are constants, where *a* cannot equal zero.

For example:

$$f(x) = x^2 - 4x + 2.$$

Can be asserted in Prolog as:

```
quad(X,Y):- Y is X*X - 4*X + 2.
```

It is queried as:

```
?- quad(2,Y).
Y = -2
?- quad(0,Y).
Y = 2.
```

This approach can be used whenever there is an *algebraic* definition available for a mathematical function.

Trigonometric functions (*sine, cosine, and tangent*) are based on the geometry of a triangle. To evaluate the trigonometric functions, series can be used. For example:

$$sine(x) = x - \frac{x^3}{3!} + \frac{x^5}{5!} - \frac{x^7}{7!} + ...$$

The first three terms can be asserted in Prolog as:

```
sine(X,Y):-
    Y is X-(X^3)/(3*2*1)+(X^5)/(5*4*3*2*1).
```

To find the *sine* of *1 radian*, the following query can be made:

```
?- sine(1,Y).
Y = 0.8416666666
```

Similarly:

$$cosine(x) = 1 - \frac{x^2}{2!} + \frac{x^4}{4!} - \frac{x^6}{6!} + ...$$

As more terms are added to these series, the accuracy of the result is improved. When written in this form, the functions can easily be defined, using the basic Prolog arithmetic predicates.

For these formulae to work, angles must be expressed in radians. (360 degrees = 2π radians).

The values of *tangent(x)*, *secant(x)* and *cosecant(x)* can also be found from the above series since,

$$tangent(x) = \frac{sine(x)}{cosine(x)}$$

$$secant(x) = \frac{1}{cosine(x)}$$

$$cosecant(x) = \frac{1}{sine(x)}$$

Exponential and *logarithmic* functions are also best evaluated using the appropriate series:

$$e^x = 1 + \frac{x}{1!} + \frac{x^2}{2!} + \frac{x^3}{3!} + \dots$$

$$ln/1 + x/ = x - \frac{x^2}{2} + \frac{x^3}{3} - \frac{x^4}{4} + \dots$$

Other logarithmic series are also available, more suited to specific applications. These can be found in most intermediate mathematics textbooks.

Mathematical Functions Exercise

For the following, the reader is expected to create programs which are able to do the calculations specified.

1. Evaluate:

$$f(x) = x^3 + 2x$$

for $x = 3$.

2. The mean of a set of numbers is obtained by adding them together, and then dividing them by the total number of figures. Calculate the mean of the following set of integers:

$$1,3,5,3,6,7,3,7,2,3.$$

3. Evaluate:

$$sine(x) + cosine(x) + tangent(x)$$

when $x = 30$ degrees.

4. The formula:

$$x = \frac{-b +/- (b^2 - 4ac)^{1/2}}{2a}$$

is used to find the roots (possible values of *x*) of the quadratic equation:

$$ax^2 + bx + c = 0$$

Design a program to solve quadratic equations, and then use it to solve the equation:

$$4x^2 + 4x - 3 = 0$$

5. Design a program, using the recursive definition for the terms of the exponential series, to evaluate the value of *e* to any suitable degree of accuracy.

6.5   *Mathematical Operations*

Another mathematical operation which will be looked at here is that of *matrix addition*. A matrix is an array of values, constants or variables, or both, such that each element is independent of the others. The position of the individual *elements* in the matrix, generally has significance with regard to the interpretation of the matrix. Addition, subtraction, and multiplication of matrices is possible. Here is a matrix *M*:

$$M = \begin{vmatrix} 5 & 4 \\ 3 & 2 \end{vmatrix}$$

Here is another matrix *N*:

$$N = \begin{vmatrix} 3 & 5 \\ 0 & 4 \end{vmatrix}$$

If these are added, to get *M* + *N*, corresponding elements are added:

$$M + N = \begin{vmatrix} 5+3 & 4+5 \\ 3+0 & 2+4 \end{vmatrix} = \begin{vmatrix} 8 & 9 \\ 3 & 6 \end{vmatrix}$$

The elements are said to be in *rows* and *columns*. Thus the element of matrix *M* which is in row *1* and column *2* is the number *4*. Two elements can only be added if their corresponding row and column numbers are equal. The element of the result has the same row and column numbers, as the elements which were added. A predicate `matrix(Name,Row,Column,Value)` can be defined to designate the value of the element, in a specified row and column of a particular named matrix. A suitable program for adding two matrices is given here:

```
%    matrix addition

%    matrix details
matrix('M',1,1,5).
matrix('M',1,2,4).
```

```
matrix('M',2,1,3).
matrix('M',2,2,2).
matrix('N',1,1,3).
matrix('N',1,2,5).
matrix('N',2,1,0).
matrix('N',2,2,4).

%   rule for adding elements
matrix_sum(Sum_Row,Sum_Column,Value):-
     matrix('M',M_Row,M_Column,M_Value),
     matrix('N',N_Row,N_Column,N_Value),
     M_Row is N_Row, M_Column is N_Column,
     Sum_Value is M_Value + N_Value.
```

Exercises on Mathematical Operations

1.Integration can be performed in Prolog using the *trapezium* rule. Write a program which will integrate any continuous function, which remains in the positive quadrant of the Cartesian plane.

2.Develop a program to carry out matrix multiplication, according to the following rule:

$$\begin{vmatrix} a & b \\ c & d \end{vmatrix} \begin{vmatrix} e & f \\ g & h \end{vmatrix} = \begin{vmatrix} ae+bg & af+bh \\ ce+dg & cf+dh \end{vmatrix}$$

6.6 Application

NEWTONIAN MECHANICS

Although Prolog is most apt for applications of some logical complexity, it can be applied both satisfactorily, and to advantage, in other domains. Many applications used with other languages are to areas of science, in which specific formulae are used to evaluate variables, given experimental and observational data. This is true of physics. For the following application, an area of physics known as *Newtonian Mechanics* is chosen. In particular, a predicate for circular motion is introduced.

The motion of a body in a circle can be given by various formulae. These relate the speed of the object, or its *tangential velocity* (v ms^{-1}), the *angular velocity* (w rads^{-1}), the *period*, or time required to complete one revolution (T secs), a *centrifugal force* (F Newtons), the *mass* of the object (m kg), the *radius* of the circle in which the object is moving (r metres), and f, the *frequency* of the movement, or the number of times it rotates in a second. Formulae connecting these variables are the following:

$$F = mv^2/r$$

$T = 1/f$
$v = rw$
$T = 2\pi/w$

The following is a starting point for this application, π has been taken as *3.142*. If the version of Prolog being used does not support decimals, use the value *3* to get an approximation.

```
%    NEWTONIAN MECHANICS- CIRCULAR MOTION
circular_motion(Force,Mass,Velocity,Radius,
     Period).
Frequency,Angular_velocity):-
     Force is Mass*Velocity*Velocity/
     Radius,
     Period is 1 / Frequency,
     Velocity is Radius * Angular Velocity,
     Period is 2 * N / w,
     N is 3.142.
```

Once developed, values for some of the variables known in a circular motions problem could be input and values of the remaining variables output.

Chapter Seven
INPUT AND OUTPUT
PREDICATES

7.1 User Interaction

Most Prolog applications involve interaction with the user. For example Prolog may display a menu of choices in response to a query and subsequently provide a chain of menus and choices as it helps the user to reach a more specific query and answer it. The way in which a program achieves this will be explained in this chapter.

User friendliness is a crucial factor in such interaction and is largely determined by the way a program looks on screen. Thus, the way in which text is handled and presented becomes important: *Is the presentation pleasing to the eye? Are the facts arranged in such a way as to be easily comprehensible?* When preparing documents and reports, printouts can often be made more interesting and easier to read, just by setting them out nicely with explicit headings.

Usually, a practical Prolog program will need to directly process information, typed in at the keyboard. without requiring the user to understand or use Prolog syntax. It may therefore be desirable to design a program, which accepts commands in natural language.

It is way beyond the scope of this book to teach the art of computer text presentation and graphics. We shall, however, introduce some of the built-in predicates included with most versions of Prolog, which are available for presentation and handling of text.

The terms *output stream* and *input stream* in the following sections should, for the time being, be interpreted as the computer terminal's screen and keyboard respectively. These terms do actually have more general meanings, which are discussed towards the end of this chapter.

7.2 write(term) and read(term)

The predicate `write(term)` causes a term to be written to the current output stream. If `term` is an uninstantiated variable, it will be output as an underscore followed by a number unique to that variable (eg. _625).

Almost opposite in action to `write`, the predicate `read(term)` is used to read a term from the current input stream. If `term` is a constant, it will be matched with the input term, and `read` will succeed or fail, depending on whether they match or not. This predicate expects a term as input, exactly as in a rule, with quotes and final full stop. If `term` is a variable, it will be instantiated to the input term. If the end of the current input stream has been reached, `term` will instead be instantiated to the atom `end_of_file`.

Examples on write(term) and read(term)

The following program allows interaction with a database, in a way which makes use of the text predicates `read` and `write`.

```
position(jones, director).
position(rogers, supervisor).
find_position:-
    read(Input),position(Input,Output),
    write(Output).
?-find_position.
allen.
manager
```

Depending on the version of Prolog being used, either apostrophes have to be avoided altogether, or they have to be paired. Thus `Kevins hat` and `Kevin''s hat` are acceptable, but `Kevin's hat` is not.

The next example is a program containing a database of the positions and names of staff in a small company. It can be used to query the position of a specified member of the company, given their name:

```
position(jones, director).
position(allen, manager).
position(rogers, supervisor).
find_position:-
    write('Whose position do you wish to
    know?'),
    read(Input), position(Input, Output),
    write('The position of '), write(Input),
    write(' is '), write(Output), write('.').
```

To run the program, enter:

```
find_position.
```

Prolog will ask:

```
Whose position do you wish to know?
```

Enter, for example:

```
allen.
```

Prolog answers with:

```
        The position of allen is manager
```
Here is another example of an interactive program. It uses quotes, so that capital letters can be used when grammatically correct. It is however necessary, for user responses to be enclosed in single quotes. The purpose of this program is to prompt the user for the name of a country, and to then find its capital.

```
        capital('England', 'London').
        capital('France', 'Paris').
        capital('Eire', 'Dublin').
        know_capital:-
            write('Give me the name of a country.
            Enclose the name in single quotes'),
            read(Country),
            capital(Country, Capital),
            write('The capital of '),
            write(Country),write('is '),
            write(Capital), write('.').
```
Query:
```
        ?-   know_capital.
        Give me the name of a country. Enclose the
        name in single quotes.
```
Enter, for example:
```
        'France'.
```
Prolog answers:
```
        The capital of France is Paris.
```

write(term) and read(term) Exercise

1) Write a program using the read and write predicates, to find the class in which each of the following persons belong:

Johnson 2A	Morris 3B
Austen 1C	Smith 4F
Harrison 3B	Audley 1C

2) Write a question and answer program, which will give the names for polygons with varying numbers of sides.

7.3 get(Ascii), get0(Ascii) and put(Ascii)

The get0(Ascii) predicate is used to read a single character from the current input stream. If Ascii is a constant then an attempt is made to match it with the next input character. Otherwise if Ascii is a variable, it will be instantiated to the ASCII value of that character.

A similar predicate get(Ascii) will ignore any non-printable characters, before reading the next printable character. A printable character is one with an ASCII value between 33 and 126 inclusive. Notice that ASCII code 32 (the SPACE character) is ignored. Thus, one of the uses of get could be to close unnecessary spaces in a text. Here are some examples using get. First, to ask what is the next input character ASCII code:

```
?-  get(Next_ASCII).
```

Input, for example:

```
a
```

Prolog responds:

```
Next_ASCII = 97
```

To ask whether the next character at User's input has ASCII code, say, 97:

```
?-  get(97).
a.
```

Prolog confirms:

```
yes
```

Conversely:

```
?-  get(98).
a.
no
```

The predicate put(Ascii) writes the character with ASCII code Ascii, to the current output stream. To write ASCII 97 or 'a':

```
?-  put(97).
a
```

Here Prolog is asked to repeat the User's input:

```
?-  get(Next_ASCII), put(Next_ASCII).
a.
```

Prolog repeats:

```
a
Next_ASCII = 97
```

This short program will change a lower case letter input to an upper case letter output:

```
?-  get(Next_ASCII), put(Capital_ASCII),
    Capital_ASCII is Next_ASCII - 32.
```

Input:

```
a.
```

Output

```
A
Next_ASCII = 97
Capital_ASCII = 65
```

7.4 tab(I) and nl

It can hardly be ignored, that although the previous interactive programs worked, the display was messy. Prolog has built-in predicates capable of tab(I) and nl   77

starting new lines and indenting text.

The `tab(I)` predicate writes I number of spaces (ASCII code 32) to the current output stream. nl which has no argument, generates a new line character.

This program uses `tab` and `nl` to set out a table.

```
table:- (tab(33), write('TABLE'), nl, nl,
tab(20), write('Surname'), tab(18),
write('First name'), nl,
tab(20), write('James'), tab(20),
write('Chris'),nl, tab(20),
write('Smithson'),tab(17),write('Susan'),
nl,
tab(20),
write('Rogers'), tab(19), write('Roy')), nl.
table.% Run Program
```

```
                TABLE


Surname            First name
James              Chris
Smithson           Susan
Rogers             Roy
```

The next example displays a menu of choices for the user.

```
menu:-
        write('Which of the following courses are
        you interested in?'), nl, nl, tab(7),
        write('1.MATHEMATICS.'), nl, tab(7),
        write('2.COMPUTING.'), nl, tab(7),
        write('3.PHYSICS.'), nl, nl,
        write('Please enter your choice
        here...').
?-  menu.
```

```
Which of the following courses are you interested
in?

        1.MATHEMATICS.
        2.COMPUTING.
        3.PHYSICS.
    Please enter your choice here...
```

tab and nl Exercise

1) Use the `tab` predicate to make up a table displaying the following information as a pair of vertical columns.

Day:	Mon.	Tue.	Wed.	Thu.	Fri.	Sat.	Sun.
Max Temp:	12	14	16	19	18	18	18
Min Temp:	3	4	2	4	6	5	0

2) Write a program to create a menu for a travel agency, showing a choice of possible destinations.

7.5 name(atom,code)

It may be necessary to convert the characters which constitute an atom, into their corresponding ASCII codes. This can be useful for applications, designed to sort atoms alphabetically, since the sorting can then be carried out numerically.

The built-in predicate `name(atom,code)` is designed for such purposes. Conversely, ASCII codes can also be converted back to atoms by using the name predicate.

name Examples

```
?-    name(wild,Code).
      Code = [119][105][108][100]
?-    name(Atom, [120,121,122]).
      Atom = xyz
```

7.6 Using Data Files

All data input to Prolog is read from an input stream, which is usually the keyboard. However it is possible to redirect the process, so that input is taken a file. The output stream (usually the screen) can also be redirected *to* a file.

It is in fact possible to use all of the predicates mentioned previously in this chapter, with files as the input and output streams. With this being the case, it is possible to process separate files, containing data. This data can be anything from a database, to a letter needing grammatical correction from Prolog.

Another use for this feature is that of temporary storage, where text could be stored for later referral in a program.

7.7 Controlling the Input and Output Streams

To redirect the input and output streams from the user to a file, the programmer has access to several built-in predicates.

The `see` and `seen` predicates will respectively open and close a file, to be read from. For example, to open the data file `Addresses`, the following would be used:

```
?- see('Addresses').
```

The predicates already mentioned in this chapter can then be used to read and process information from this file.

```
?- seen.
```

will close `Addresses` and redirect input, to come from the user.

Alternatively,

```
?- see(user).
```

The predicates `tell` and `told` enable information to be output to a file. Therefore the following commands could be used to open and close the file `accounts`.

```
?- tell(accounts).
```

and then

```
?- told.
```

or

```
?- tell(user).
```

Two extra predicates are supplied with some versions of Prolog. `telling(Name)` and `seeing(Name)` will instantiate the names of the current files being output and input, to the variable Name. Therefore, if these predicates were used, whilst the files used in the previous examples were open, something similar to the following would be seen on the screen:

```
?- seeing(Reading).
   Reading = Addresses
```

and

```
?- telling(Output_Stream).
   Output_Stream = accounts
```

Input and Output Streams Examples

Using a text editor, write the following program. First, open file `Message` for input:

```
?- tell('Message').
```

Now write this to output stream:

```
?- write('Hello Reader!').
```

Next close the output stream:

```
?- told.
```

Then write the following to the output stream:

```
?- write('Hello Reader!').
```

Save this as `IO_EXAMP` and then run it from Prolog by entering,

```
[IO_EXAMP].
```

The message `Hello Reader!` will appear on the screen. However, a file called `Message` has also been created. If this is inspected using a text editor, the reader will find that this also contains the message.

Input and Output Streams Exercise

Design a program which can take a sentence of upper and lower case letters, and convert them all to lower case. A use of this would be to enable upper and lower case data, to be compared with a database of lower case data. Here are some hints as to how the program could be structured:

1. Use get0(Code) to read in each character as ASCII.
2. If Code is less than or equal to 90 (ASCII code for Z), and greater than or equal to 65 (ASCII A), then add 32 to that value. (To make it lower case.)
3. Output value to a file, using put.
4. Repeat to line 1, until end_of_file is instantiated for Code.
5. The new file created, can then be used as the current input stream, and used by whatever application needs the sentence in lower case.

Chapter Eight
DATA STRUCTURES

8.1 Introduction

Most computer languages will only directly accept data as individual items of information. However, Prolog will accept structured data, complete with relations. In this way, real life situations can be more readily and more accurately modelled in the computer program. Not only this, programs can be more modular, which makes them more compact and more easily understood, an advantage especially important for lengthy programs.

In this chapter a number of different ways of presenting data in Prolog are presented. Applications of each are also given. Some of these structures and applications are particularly important in artificial intelligence. Thus, Prolog programs are often designed to behave as *experts*, and to respond to queries in the same way as an expert in some subject area would. So-called *Expert Systems*.

8.2 Lists

The most basic data structure has already been mentioned in chapter four. It is the *list*. The common sense idea of a shopping list is a reasonable starting point for understanding this structure. There are no repetitions of items, or *elements* as they are called. However, unlike the shopping list, the order of the elements is important.

A list may contain only one element or none at all. The elements of lists may be of any degree of complexity, but other data structures are available in Prolog which may be more suitable, when the elements are complicated. It is possible for elements themselves to be lists.

There are different notations for lists. The square bracket notation is probably the most popular and the easiest to use. The entities `alan`, `bernice`, `christine` can then be listed as:

```
[alan, bernice, christine]
```

Other examples are:

> [x]

which has only the element x,

> []

which contains no elements, and

> [a, b, [c, d, [e, f]]]

which has lists within lists.

Lists are thought of as having a *head* and a *tail*. The head is the leftmost element of the list. The tail is the remainder of that list. This demarcation is important when recursive procedures are applied to lists. When this is the case, the head is processed in some way, and then the next element becomes a new head and is similarly processed. This process recurs until the entities of the list are exhausted.

The head and tail of a list can be kept separate by a | symbol in square bracket notation. In general, if H stands for the head and T for the tail, the list is denoted as [H | T].

To understand the method used by Prolog to examine a list, refer to Figure *8.1*. Here the list [alan|bernice,christine] is being examined, an element at a time. The list can be visualised as a tree, where its branches repeatedly split into two. This is an example of a *binary tree*. The elements are considered one at a time, starting from the left of the list. Accordingly the analysis of the list is *deterministic*, and follows a fixed pattern.

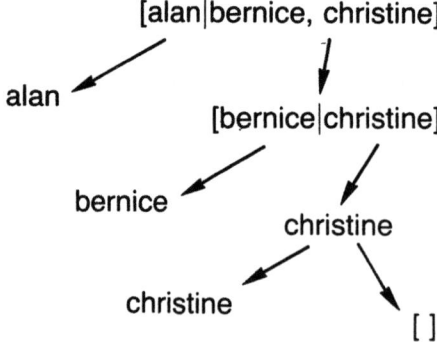

Figure. 8.1

Lists Examples

1)Assert:

```
family([chris, janet, martin, david]).
?- family(All).
All = [chris, janet, martin, david]
?- family([Head | Rest]).
Head = chris
Rest = [janet, martin, david]
?- family([Dad, Mum |Kids]).
Dad = chris
Mum = janet
Kids = [martin, david]
?- family([Head | _]).
Head = chris
?- family([ _, [Head | Rest]]).
no
```

Here is an example of a more complex list structure.

```
time_table
    ([Class,[Period,Subject],Teacher]).
time_table
    ([class_one,[first_period,maths].jones]).
time_table
    ([class_one,[second_period,french],miles]).
time_table
    ([class_two,[first_period,art],golding]).
time_table
    ([class_two,[second_period,maths],cutting]).
```

This can be queried, for example, to find who teaches maths:

```
?- time_table([_,[_,maths],Teacher]).
Teacher = jones ;
Teacher = cutting ;
no
```

Here is another query to find which subjects are being taught in which periods:

```
?- time_table([_,[Period,Subject],_]).
Period = first_period
```

```
Subject = maths ;
Period = second_period
Subject = french ;
Period = first_period
Subject = art ;
Period = second_period
Subject = maths ;
no
```

Lists Exercise

Assert:

```
drivers([ alan, bert, charles, desmond]).
loaders([ alfonso, bob, chris, derek]).
```

Predict how Prolog will respond to these queries:

1. `?-loaders([Foreman | Gang]).`
2. `?-drivers([_ | Team]).`
3. `?-drivers([Foreman, Supervisor | Others]).`
4. `?-loaders(All).`
5. `?-loaders([Foreman, bob, chris, Student]).`
6. `?-drivers(All, Sundry).`

8.3 Operations on Lists

There many operations which can be carried out on lists of elements. These include concatenating, amending, checking membership, counting list length, reversal of a list and finding the nth member.

The predicate =.., pronounced *univ* provides a way of displaying and checking the arguments of a given predicate. It provides a list composed of the predicate and its arguments. Alternatively, it will check whether a given predicate has specified arguments.

When using univ, the predicate `call(goal)` will often also be needed (this succeeds if an attempt to satisfy `goal` succeeds). It has the same effect as asking the database the question `goal`. The reason for using this apparently redundant predicate, is that a difficulty can arise in some versions of Prolog, where `goal` is syntactically an atom or similar. This prevents variables from being accepted as goals. Using `call(goal)`, a predicate may be queried even if it is uninstantiated during a search. This is sometimes called a *meta-variable* facility.

List Operations Examples

Many of the following user-defined predicates are available as built-in predicates. Nonetheless it is worth following the examples through, so as to improve your knowledge of the way in which recursive definitions work on lists. Also, the basic recursive strategy is adaptable to an endless variety of situations, where data appears as lists, and lists within lists.

Two lists can be joined together (*concatenated*) using the procedure:

```
join([],S,S). % clause 1
join([H|S],T,[H|W]):- join(S,T,W). % clause 2
```

For example:

```
?-join
    ([alan,bernice,christine],
    [dave,eric,fred],New_list).

New_list=
    [alan,bernice,christine,dave,eric,fred]
```

The procedure works in the following way: The head of the first list is removed by the first clause. Then `alan` is removed, followed by `bernice` and then `christine`. Termination of this occurs when there is a match with clause 1. At this stage, the last head to be removed from the first list, becomes the head of the result. Successive heads are thus added to the resultant list.

An element can be removed from a list using the following procedure:

```
remove(S,[S|T],L):- remove(S,T,L),!.
remove(S,[S|T],T).
remove(S,[U|T],[U|L]):- remove(S,T,L).
```

For example:

```
?-  remove
    (alan,[alan,bernice,christine],New_list)
New_list = [bernice,christine]
```

The *length* of a list can be found by using the procedure:

```
length([],0).
length([S|T],M):- length(T,N),M is N + 1.
```

For example:

```
?-  length([alan,bernice,christine],Length).
Length = 3

?-  length([[alan,bernice],Name],Length).

Name = _1
Length = 2
```

(The response Name = _1 is not a list length, but Prolog stating a value for an instantiated variable.)

A list can be *reversed* or checked to be the reverse of a given list, by using the next procedure:

```
reverse([],[]).
reverse([S|T],L):-reverse(T,V), join(V,[S],L).
```

(Note that use is made of the earlier list predicate join.)

For example:

```
?-  reverse
    ([alan|bernice,christine],Reverse_list).
Reverse_list = [christine,bernice,alan]
```

It is very useful to define a predicate to determine whether a given element is a *member of* a given list. Applications could include checking club membership, stock-keeping, progress chasing and so on. The following procedure is for this purpose:

```
member_of(S,[S|T]).
member_of(S,[V|T]):- member_of(S,T).
```

For example:

```
?-  member_of(bernice,
    [alan,bernice,christine]).
yes

?-  member_of(bernice,christine).
no

?-  member_of(Member,
    [alan,bernice,christine]).
Member = alan ;
Member = bernice;
Member = christine;
no
```

If the *nth member* of a list is required, the following procedure can be used.

```
nth_member(S,1,[S|_]).
nth_member
(S,N,[_|L]):-T is N - 1, nth_member(S,T,L).
```

For example:

```
?-  nth_member
    (Member,2,[alan,bernice,christine]).
Member = bernice.
```

=.. *Examples*

```
?-  parent(mary,john) =.. L.
L = [parent, john, mary]

?-  parent(Who,Whom) =.. L.
Who = _1
Whom = _2
L = [parent, _1, _2]

?-  [2, 3, 5, 7] =.. L.
L = [., 2, [3, 5, 7]]
```

Lists Operations Exercise

1. Join the list of odd numbers `[1,2,5,7]` to the list of prime numbers `[2,3,5,7]`.
2. Remove the element 3 from the list `[2,3,5,7,11,13]`.
3. Find the length of the list `[a,e,i,o,u]`.
4. Reverse the list `[a,b,c,d,e,f,g]`.
5. Check that `1973` is a member of `[1962,1932,1987,1945,1973]`.
6. Find the 3rd member of `[ab,bc,cd,de,ef,fg,gh,hi,ij]`.
7. Design a procedure to eliminate all occurrences of a particular element from a list.
8. Design a procedure to eliminate any duplication of elements in a list.
9. Design a procedure which will output the elements common to two given lists.
10. Predict what Prolog will respond to:
    a) `?-(x - y) =.. L.`
    b) `?-(x - y) =.. [_, X, Y].`
    c) `?-(x + y) =.. [_, X, x].`

Lists Applications

SORTING

A list structure lends itself well to *sorting* (for example into alphanumeric order). There are a number of strategies for sorting a list. The following method, defined by Clocksin and Mellish (1987) uses an *insertion sort*. Elements of the original list are sorted by removing them one at a time, to form a new list into which each element is inserted, in the correct order.

```
insort([],[],_).
insort([X|L],Sort_list,Ordering):-
insort(L,N,Ordering),insortx(X,N,M,Ordering).
insortx(X,[A|L],[A|M],Ordering):-
```

```
        P=..[Ordering,A,X],call(P),!,
        insortx(X,L,M,Ordering).
    insortx(X,L,[X|L],Ordering).
```

< must be substituted for `Ordering` if it is desired to sort numerically. Alternatively, the predicate `aless`, as defined below, replaces it for alphabetical sorting:

```
aless(X,Y):-name(X,L),name(Y,M),alessx(L,M).
alessx([],[_|_]).
alessx([X|_],[Y|_]):- X < Y.
alessx([H|Q],[H|S]):-alessx(Q,S).
```

INSURANCE BROKER

This case study is based on a program by Burnham and Hall (1985). It provides insurance quotes.

The predicate `response` is to provide an interactive capability for the user. *Car data* is established using the `car_group` predicate, which has as its arguments, `car_type`, `engine_size` and `insurance_group` - in that order. Basic *premiums* are given in the predicate `basic_premium` which has the arguments `group`, `cost`, `company` and `type` - again, in that order. *Company loadings* are asserted by the predicate `loading`, which is of the form,

```
loading(Company, Type[[Codes,Loadings]]).
```

The format of a *costs for extras* predicate `extras`, is the same as that of `loading`.

To use the program, the user must first enter `go`. This predicate causes the data and utility files to be consulted. Information specified by user input is then obtained using the predicate `car_details`. This allows the insurance group of the car specified to be found. The type of insurance, any extras and details of the current no claims bonus are then obtained.

The use of `cut` prevents any of this information being requested again. The cost of the insurance is then calculated, using the details given and the information on policies, listed in the database.

The predicate `fix` is used to change a decimal to an integer.

```
%    DATA
'DATA.PRO'

%    USER PROMPTS
response
    (1,['','Please enter the model of the
    clients car',
'Enclose your answer in single quotes. ']).
```

```
response
    (2,['','Please enter the engine size in
    c.c.']).
response
    (3,['','Please enter the date of
    manufacture']).
response
    (4,['','Give the clients surname and
    initials',
'Enclose your answer in single quotes']).
response(5,['','Give the clients address',
'Enclose your answer in single quotes']).
response
    (6,['','List any convictions according to
    the codes given,
'','Drink Driving..............d',
'','Dangerous Driving.........dd',
'','Speeding...................s',
'Enter as a list']).
response(7,['','What is the clients age?']).
response(8,['','What type of insurance?',
'','Third party fire and theft........tpft',
'','Full
    comprehensive.................fcomp']).
response
    (9,['','Please enter any extras according
    to the
    following codes',
'','Protected Policy(full comp. only)......p',
'','Windscreen Insurance....................w',
'','Radio/Cassette insurance..............r',
'','Enter as a list']).
response
    (10,['What is the clients no-claim bonus
    in % ?']).

%   CAR DATA
car_group('ford cortina',2000,5).
car_group('mini metro',1300,3).
car_group('mini metro',1100,2).
car_group('MG metro',1300,4).

%   BASIC PREMIUMS
```

```
basic_premium
    (2,100,'Cheap Insurance PLC',tpft).
basic_premium(2,250,'Pricey Insurance',fcomp).
basic_premium
    (2,150,'Cheap Insurance PLC',fcomp).
basic_premium
    (3,349,'Cheap Insurance PLC',fcomp).
basic_premium(3,245,'Cheap Insurance',tpft).
basic_premium(3,400,'Pricey Insurance',fcomp).
basic_premium(3,275),'Pricey Insurance',tpft).

%    COMPANY LOADINGS
loading('PriceyInsurance',
    tpft,[[d,300],[s,45],[dd,50]]).
loading('Pricey Insurance',
    fcomp,[[d,350],[s,45],[dd,50]]).
loading('Cheap Insurance PLC',
    tpft,[[d,400],[s,30],[dd,80]]).

%    COSTS FOR EXTRAS
extras('Pricey Insurance',
    fcomp,[[p,25],w,25],[r,30]]).
extras('Pricey Insurance',
    tpft,[[r,30],[w,35]]).
extras('Cheap Insurance PLC',
    fcomp,[[p,25],[w,35],[r,20]]).
extras('Cheap Insurance PLC',
    tpft,[[r,25],[w,35]]).

%    UTILITIES
'UTIL.PRO'

%    FINDING LOADINGS AND EXTRAS
calculate_loading(Options,Data,Results):-
calculate_loading(Options,Data,0,Result).
calculate_loading([],_,N,N).
calculate_loading
    ([Option|Rest],Data,N,Total):-
    entry(Option,Data,Value),
    Sum is N + Value,
    calculate_loading(Rest,Data,Sum,Total).
entry(H,[[H,Y]|_],Y):-!.
entry(H,[_|T],P):-entry(H,T,P).

%    FINDING THE LENGTH OF A LIST
```

```
length(X,J):-flen(X,J,0),
    flen([],Y,Y).
flen([H|T],Y,Z):-P is Z + 1, flen(T,Y,P).

%   INPUT OUTPUT PROCEDURE
inp_outp(resp(R,X),Y):-
    call(resp(R,X)), screen(X), nl,
    write('|:'), read(Y).
screen([]):- !.
screen([H|T]):-write(H), nl, screen(T).

%   CONSULT FILES
'CONS.PRO'

%   READ IN DATA FILE AND UTILITY PROCEDURES
go:- consult('data.pro'),
    consult('util.pro'),start.

%   OUTPUT TOP LINE AND GET USER INFORMATION
start:-resp(0,X),screen(X),get_car(Data),
    comput(Data).

%   GET CAR DETAILS
get_car(data_struc(A,B)):-find_car_details(B).
find_driver_details(B).
find_car_details(car_details
    (Car_make,Engine_size,Car_age)):-
    inp_outp(response(1,X),Car_make),
    inp_outp(response(2,X1),Engine_size),
    inp_outp(response(3,X2),Car_age).

%   GET DRIVER DETAILS
find_driver_details
    (driver_details(Driver, Address,
    Convictions, Age)):-
    inp_outp(response(4,X),Driver),
    inp_outp(response(5,X1),Address),
    inp_outp(response(6,X2),Convictions),
    inp_outp(response(7,X3),Age).

%   COMPUTE QUOTE
compute(data_structure(A,B)):-
    arg(1,A,Car_make),
    arg(2,A,Engine_size),
    car_group(Car_make,Engine_size,Group),
    inp_outp(response(8,X),Type),
```

```
inp_outp(response(9,X1),Extras),
inp_outp(response(10,X2),No_claims_bonus),
!,
base_premium(Group,Premium,Company,Type),
C=insurance_details
(Group,Premium,Company,Type),
D=extras_details(Extras,No_claims_bonus),
Prices(A,B,C,D),
write('Another Quote y/n: '),
read(Reply),
Res=n.
```

```
%     CALCULATE PRICES OF AVAILABLE POLICIES
prices(A,B,C,D):-
    A = car_details
    (Car_make,Engine_size,Car_age),
    B = driver_details
    (Driver,Address,Convictions,Age),
    C=insurance_details
    (Group,Premium,Company,Type),
    D = extras_details
    (Extras,No_claims_bonus),
    loading(Company,Type,Loading),
    calculate_loading(Convictions,Loading,Y),
    length(Convictions,J),
    Loading is fix(Premium*(Y/(J*100))),
    find_extra
    (Extra_cost,Type,Company,Premium,Extras),
    discounts(Discount,Car_age,Age,E),
    calculate_discount(Discount,Premium,E,N),
    output
    (Driver,Address,Car_make,Engine_size,
    Car_age,Age,Group,Company,Type,
    Premium,Loading,Extra_cost,N,
    No_claims_bonus),
    nl, nl, !.
```

```
%     FIND EXTRAS REQUIRED AND THEIR COST
find_extra(B,Type,Company,Premium,Extra):-
    extras(Company,Type,Xtra),
    calculate_loading(Extra,Xtra,Y),
    length(Extra,H),
    B is fix(Premium*(Y/(H*100))).
```

```
%    CALCULATE DISCOUNTS
discounts(Discount,Car_age,Age,E):-
    car_age_discount(CCar_age,V,S),
    age_discount(Age,U,P),
    Discount is U + V,
    Q is S + P,
    ((Q = 0, E = 1, !);E = Q.
car_age_discount
    (Car_age,10,1):-1985 - Car_age >= 10, !.
car_age_discount(_,0,0).
age_discount(Age,25,1):- Age >= 25, !.
age_discount(_,0,0).
cdis(Dis,Prem,E,N):-
    N is fix(Prem*(Dis/E*100))).

%    OUTPUT FORMATTING
output
    (Driver,Address,Car_make,Engine_size,
    Car_age,Age,Group,
    Type,Premium,Loading,B,N,
    No_claims_bonus):-
    write('Insurance Quotation: '),nl,
    write
    ('Drivers Name............'),
    write(Driver),nl,
    write
    ('Drivers Age.............'),
    write(Age),nl,
    write
    ('Address.................'),
    write(Address),nl,
    write
    ('Insurance Company........'),
    write(Company),nl,
    write
    ('Insurance Type...........'),
    write(Type),nl,
    write
    ('Vehicle Type.............'),
    write(Car_make),nl,tab(2)
    write(Engine_size),nl,
    write
```

```
('Date of manufacture......'),
write(Car_age),nl,
write
('Insurance Group..........'),
write(Group),nl,
write
('Basic Premium............'),
write(Premium),nl,
write
('Extras Requested.........'),
write(B),nl,
write('Loadings.................'),
write(Loading),nl,
write('Discounts................'),
write(N),nl,
write('No claims bonus..........'),
write(No_claims_bonus),
write('%'),nl,
Cost is fix((Premium + B + Loading
- N * (No_claims_bonus/100))),
write('Amount payable is........'),
write(Cost),nl.
```

8.4 Semantic Networks

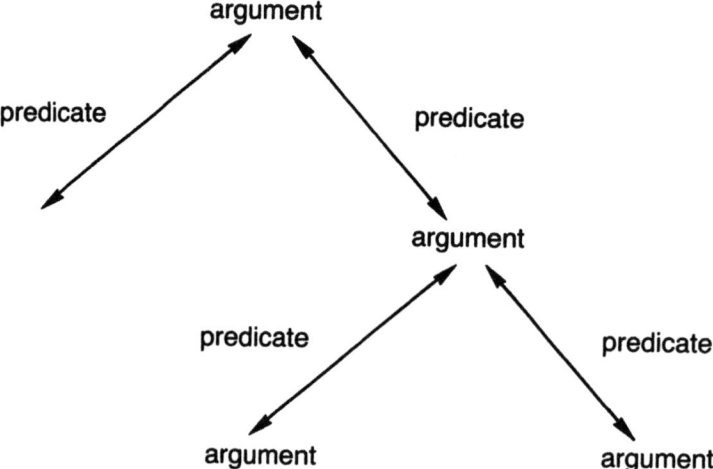

Figure 8.2

Generally speaking, the relations and objects represented by the predicates and their arguments in Prolog, can be drawn as a network of lines and their intersections. (See Figure 8.2). Such a diagram represents the *meaning* of the data structure, and is called a *semantic network*.

The lines, or *arcs* represent predicates, and the dots, or *nodes* represent their arguments. Some knowledge structures lend themselves well to such an approach. Included among these are many scientific theories. On the other hand, when predicates have many arguments, the corresponding increase in the numbers of arcs may only lead to a confusing maze!

Semantic Networks Example

Here is an example of the use of semantic networks, as derived from the science of biology. It concerns the classification, or *taxonomy* of living organisms. The different classes used are animal or plant, vertebrate or non-vertebrate, and flowering or non-flowering. Here are the rules which apply:

1.   A life-form is either an *animal* or a *plant*.
2.   A life-form *feeds*, *respires*, *replicates* and *grows*.
3.   An animal either has a vertebral column, or it does not. If it does, it
      is a *vertebrate*. If not, it is an *invertebrate*.
4.   An animal *moves*.
5.   Plants are either *flowering* or *non-flowering*.

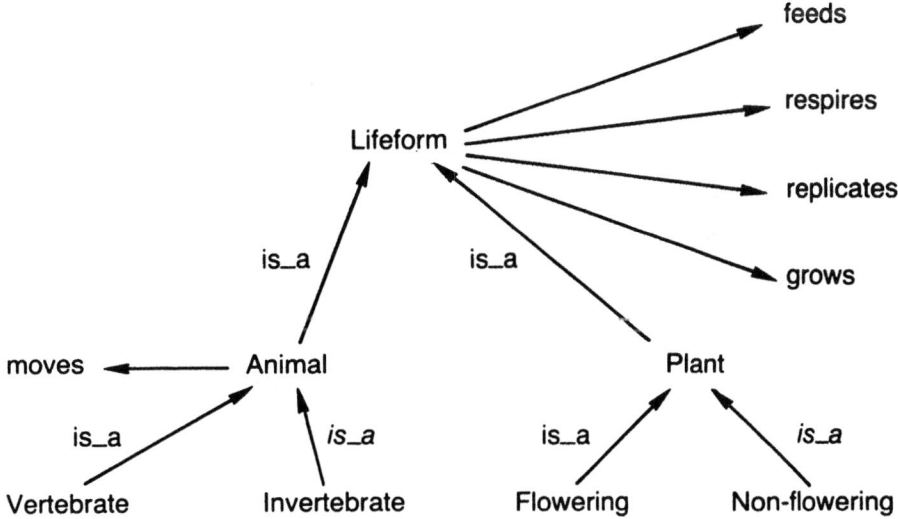

Figure 8.3

Figure *8.3* shows the semantic network for this theory. The predicate is_a should be interpreted as a *subset* or inclusion relation, rather than a *membership* relation. The predicates feeds, respires, replicates, grows and moves apply to the objects from which the arrows are rooted. It is required that predicates applying to objects higher in the network, apply to objects included in those via the is_a relation. For example, if a living organism respires, then so does an animal, and so does a vertebrate. Similarly, the is_a relation is passed on in the sense that if A is_a B, and B is_a C then A is_a C. In a word, it is *transitive*. However, beware of trying to define such inheritance, using the transitivity relations of the logic chapter. If it is simply translated into Prolog, non-terminating rules will result. Instead, it must be programmed recursively, in this case using an additional subset predicate.

```
%    Life_Taxonomy
is_a(animal,life_form).
is_a(plant,life_form).
is_a(vertebrate,animal).
is_a(invertebrate,animal).
is_a(flower,plant).
is_a(flowerless,plant).

feeds(life_form).
respires(life_form).
replicates(life_form).
grows(life_form).
moves(animal).

subset(X,Y):-is_a(X,Y).
subset(X,Y):-is_a(W,Y),subset(X,W).

respires(M):-subset(M,N),respires(N).
moves(P):-subset(P,Q),moves(Q).
feeds(R):-subset(R,S),feeds(S).
grows(V):-subset(V,W),replicates(U).
replicates(X):-subset(X,Y),replicates(Y).
```

For example:

```
?:- is_a(animal,life_form).
    yes

?-  moves(vertebrate).
    yes

?-  replicates(invertebrate).
```

```
            yes

?-   moves(life_form).
            no
```

If the last response seems odd, remember that this query actually asks whether *all* life-forms move. As plants do not, this cannot therefore be true.

If facts about individual living organisms are asserted, more specific questions can be asked:

```
        is_a(cat,animal).
```

Query:

```
?-   moves(cat).
        yes

?-   is_a(cat,life_form).
        no
```

The reason the program gives the wrong answer, is because the inheritance clause does not work in the correct direction, for the query to succeed. More facts about the cat would have to be asserted within the present program.

Semantic Networks Exercise

Use a sematic network to describe the parts and contents of a house. For example, the house contains a bedroom, a lounge, a kitchen etc. The bedroom contains a wardrobe, a bed, a chair, etc. The wardrobe contains a coat, a hat etc. Use the program to work out what is where in the house.

Semantic Networks Applications

GENETICS

It is possible to use Prolog, to provide expert systems for the natural sciences. In this case study, part of *genetics* is considered. Genetics is the study of the hereditary transmission of features, or *characters* in life-forms, and of the material basis for this transmission.

There are probabilistic and population studies on the one hand, such as those carried out originally by Mendel, often called *transmission genetics*. On the other hand there are *molecular* studies, such as those usually associated with Watson and Crick's double helix model for DNA.

One problem which arises when applying Prolog to the natural sciences, is that there can exist many formulations of the same subject area. In most cases the differences are superficial or even linguistic. For example, whether the characters studied in genetics are expressed in *gross* terms, such as colour, or the underlying biochemicals responsible for those colours, may be immaterial to an application of Mendelian genetics. It is however, essential to have an understanding of the biochemistry of a character, in order to apply molecular genetics.

The starting point for a Prolog programmer to provide an expert system of a natural science, may well be the end result of considerable mathematical, logical and even philosophical study. The following application is based on a mathematico-logico analysis of genetics. (Dawe 1982, Balzer and Dawe 1986a, Balzer and Dawe 1986b, Balzer and Dawe 1993). A schema for the structure of genetics arrived at is shown in Fig. 8.4. The part of genetics which this case study concerns, is sufficient to deal with Mendelian genetics.

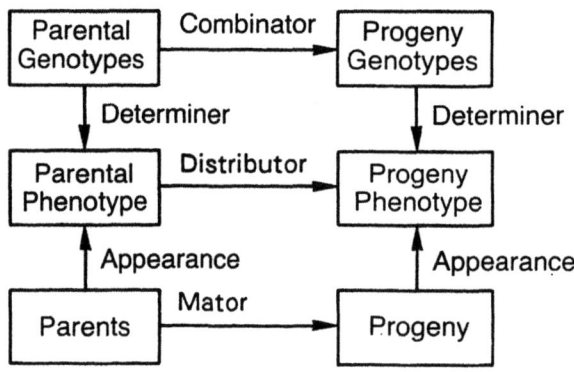

Figure 8.4

A number of genetical terms will need to be outlined. For an excellent account of undergraduate genetics, see Strickberger (1986).

Parents mate to give *progeny*. The characters of an individual or population make up its *phenotype*. The factors which cause those characters to appear rather than others, constitute the *genotype* of that individual or population. When individuals mate, characters possessed by them *may* appear in the progeny, but not necessarily. An individual receives hereditary information from *both* parents and as a result, (at least in what are called *diploid* organisms) it has two copies of the genetic information, for each of its characters. Often one of the copies will hide the effect of the other. A distinction is made between *recessive* and *dominant* genes within a genotype. Genes influencing the same character in this way are known as *alleles*, and these give rise to different *traits*. A character might be *eye colour*, while traits may be *blue eye colour* or *brown eye colour*. An individual might carry both genes for the same eye colour, or one of each. When that individual mates with another, there is a rearrangement of the genes, which will determine the genotype of the progeny.

The phenotype of the parents does not give the phenotype of the progeny. The genotype of the parents must be known, and then a list of *possible* progeny genotypes can be arrived at. A *probability* for each progeny genotype can be arrived at, through an interplay of experiment and theory which is frequently quite tortuous. The genotype carries two alleles for each character. If one allele is dominant to another, then only if it is absent altogether, will the other recessive genes operate and give the corresponding character trait.

The two alleles are inherited independently of each other, according to the *Mendelian law of independent segregation*. Accordingly, the probability that a progeny will contain alleles of any of the kinds present in either parent is equal. When more than one character is involved, the genes are inherited independently according to the *law of independent assortment*.

Returning to Fig. 8.4, the observational starting point for an application of Mendelian genetics, would concern a relation between a parent population and a progeny population. This is the relation `mator` which maps mating pairs from the parental population, to individuals in the progeny population. The population does not have to consist of individuals existing together at the same time, but may be an abstraction from observations of many individuals or populations. The `mator` function is defined here to map onto individual progenys. For example:

```
mator(jim, mary, fred).
```

means that Jim and Mary mated to give Fred.

The actual identity of the individuals of the parental and progeny populations, is secondary to the characters possessed by those individuals. The phenotypes are given by an `appearance` function. For example:

```
appearance(jim, blue_eyes).
appearance(mary, brown_eyes).
appearance(fred, blue_eyes).
```

This means that Jim has the phenotypic trait blue eyes, Mary has brown eyes, and Fred has blue eyes.

In the following, *A* is used to denote a dominant allele and *a* to denote the recessive allele. If two parents mate and each has one of each allele, the following possibilities exist for the genotypes of progeny:

Aa X Aa -> AA, Aa, aA, aa.

According to the law of independent segregation, these outcomes are equally likely, and the probability of each genotype occurring is *0.25*. Thus:

p(AA) = 0.25
p(Aa) = 0.25

$$p(aA) = 0.25$$
$$p(aa) = 0.25$$

The `combinator` function maps parent genotypes to progeny genotypes and corresponding probabilities. Thus, the predicate `combinator` can take the form:

```
combinator
    (blue_gene,brown_gene,
    blue_gene,brown_gene,
    blue_gene, blue_gene,
    blue_gene, brown_gene,
    brown_gene, blue_gene,
    brown_gene, brown_gene,
    25, 25, 25, 25).
```

Here the blue gene/brown gene and blue gene/brown gene parents, have given rise to the progeny with genotypes blue gene/blue gene, blue gene/brown gene, brown gene/blue gene, brown gene/brown gene, with corresponding probabilities of 25% for each progeny genotype.

The parental and progeny genotypes can be related back to phenotypes by the `determiner` predicate. This takes the allelic pair of an individual, and states the phenotypic trait which will result. For example:

```
determiner(blue_gene, blue_gene, blue_eyes).
determiner(blue_gene, brown_gene, brown_eyes).
determiner(brown_gene, blue_gene, brown_eyes).
determiner
    (brown_gene, brown_gene, brown_eyes).
```

The above states that an individual with two genes for blue eyes will have blue eyes. However, individuals with one gene for each will have brown eyes, as will those with two genes for brown eyes.

Finally, a function `distributor` maps the observed or expected parental phenotypes onto observed, or expected progeny phenotypes. The distributor also includes the experimental probability that each kind of phenotype, will occur in the progeny population. For example:

```
distributor
    (blue_eyes, brown_eyes,blue_eyes,
    brown_eyes, 0.74, 0.76).
```

Here, a blue eyed parent and a brown eyed parent (or parent population) have given rise to 74% blue eyed and 26% brown-eyed progeny. This does not exactly match the 3:1 ratio expected from Mendelian genetics. In practice, a range of the values for the last two arguments would be acceptable. In the following program, a range of 10% has been allowed.

The network of functions in the above model for genetics, indicates that a geneticist may start from many points. The entire rule defines `Mendelian_genetics`. If the user puts sufficient experimental or observational information into the program to fill all arguments, the program will decide whether Mendelian genetics is appropriate; it will say that Mendelian genetics is the correct explanation for the phenomena. If it is, the user may continue to use Mendelian genetics for that class of application, when some of the information is absent, and thus predict arguments which are missing.

The program consists of two files. The first contains the theory. The second contains the data. It is applied to a repeat of Mendel's experiment on seed shapes, performed by Hurst. During this *1335* smooth seeds and *420* wrinkled were obtained in the progeny. This gives *76.1%* smooth and *23.9%* wrinkled, which has been rounded to *76%* and *24%* respectively.

The data program could be extended to be interactive, so that new applications could be made more easily.

```
/* MENDELIAN GENETICS THEORY FILE */
mendelian_genetics:-
mator(Parent_A, Parent_B, Progeny_X),
appearance(Parent_A, Appearance_A),
appearance(Parent_B, Appearance_B),
appearance(Progeny_X, Appearance_X),
appearance(Progeny_Y, Appearance_Y),
combinator
     (Parent_A_allele_1, Parent_A_allele_2,
Parent_B_allele_1, Parent_B_allele_2,
     Progeny_X_allele_1, Progeny_X_allele_2,
Progeny_Y_allele_1, Progeny_Y_allele_2,
Progeny_Z_allele_1, Progeny_Z_allele_2,
Progeny_W_allele_1, Progeny_W_allele_2,
     25, 25, 25, 25),
determiner(Dom_allele, Dom_allele, Dom_trait),
determiner(Dom_allele, Rec_allele, Dom_trait),
determiner(Rec_allele, Dom_allele, Dom_trait),
determiner(Rec_allele, Rec_allele, Rec_trait),
distributor(Appearance_A, Appearance_B,
Appearance_X, Appearance_Y,
     Percentage_X, Percentage_Y),
Percentage_X > 20,
Percentage_X < 30,
Percentage_Y > 70,
     Percentage_Y < 80.
```

```
/* MENDELIAN GENETICS DATA FILE */
appearance(Parent_A, smooth).
appearance(Parent_B, wrinkled).
appearance(Progeny_X, smooth).
appearance(Progeny_Y, wrinkled).
combinator(smooth_allele, wrinkled_allele,
    smooth_allele, wrinkled_allele,
    smooth_allele, smooth_allele,
    smooth_allele, wrinkled_allele,
    wrinkled_allele, smooth_allele,
    wrinkled_allele, wrinkled_allele,
     25, 25, 25, 25).
determiner
    (smooth_allele, smooth_allele, smooth).
determiner
    (smooth_allele, wrinkled_allele, smooth).
determiner
    (wrinkled_allele, smooth_allele, smooth).
determiner
    (wrinkled_allele, wrinkled_allele,
    wrinkled).
distributor
    (smooth, wrinkled, smooth, wrinkled,
    76, 24).
```

Query:

```
?- mendelian_genetics.
   yes
```

Hurst's repeat was consistent with Mendelian genetics within the range of accuracy given here.

8.5 Frames

Sometimes it might be required to create a data structure which is common to a whole range of applications, but which varies in *detail*. For instance, the details of meetings may vary as to their date, location and purpose, so only those three parameters need to be recorded. The structure required is then like a *frame* with *slots* - one for each fact, whether date, location or purpose. The frame itself is like an abstract skeleton.

The notion of frames is developed further than this, however. Each slot can itself be a frame with its own slots. Thus taking the previous example, the date information may have slots for the date, as well as the time of the day.

The properties of the previous slot are *inherited* by the new frame, and its slots.

Frames Example

Here is a example of how such a data structure might be used. The predicate `kind_of(This,That)` implies that `This` *is a* `kind_of` `That`. More technically, `This` is a subset of `That`. The predicate `kind_of` is used here, to define a procedure for a form of inheritance.

```
%    FRAMES EXAMPLE
kind_of(rhombus,quadrilateral).
kind_of(square,rhombus).

%    SLOT VALUES SPECIAL FOR RHOMBUS
rhombus(sides,equal).
rhombus(angles,unequal).

%    SLOT VALUES SPECIAL TO SQUARE
square(symmetry,4).

%    INHERITANCE RULE
square(Attribute,Value):-
    kind_of(Square,Frame),
Subgoal =..[Frame,Attribute,Value],
    Subgoal.
```

Query:

```
?-  rhombus(sides, What).
    What = equal
```

This is what would be expected since this fact is in the database.
However query:

```
?-  square(sides, What).
    What = equal
```

Here, the property that the sides of a square are equal has been inherited from the assertion for the rhombus due to the action of the `kind_of` predicate.

Frames Exercise

1. Use a frame data structure, to write a Prolog program which will describe aspects of a motor car, which might be important for a garage. The following is an outline of one possible structure, including the use, weight, type, number of doors, price, colour, make and serial number:

```
Frame: car
```

```
a_kind_of_vehicle
use: passenger_transport
weight: light.
Frame: sports
a_kind_of: car
body: five-door
Frame: ford
a_kind_of: saloon
price: medium
colours_available: all.
Frame: 'S1763/97'
instance_of: ford
price_code: 'C'
colour: red.
```

2. Sketch a frame structure to describe staff meetings held at a company.
   The meetings held are either *staff-management*, *staff-union* or *other*.
   The staff-management meetings are held in the boardroom at 1pm.
   The staff-union meetings are held in the canteen at 1pm.
   Other meetings are held in the canteen at 1pm.
   A staff-management meeting is called with Schwartz, Petrelli, Santos and
   Christie present, to discuss proposed redundancies.

Application

TRAVEL AGENT

This application concerns a program, which will act in some respects as a
travel agent (Mellish, 1985). The program interfaces with the user, asking for
his or her travel requirements. At the same time, it makes information
available to the user, so that choices can be made. The program is intelligent
enough to avoid asking for information which the user has already given,
even if done implicitly. It can also cope with the situation where the user's
choice changes.

The predicate flight(F,T,D,Ti,Fl) states that flight number Fl is
from F to T in month D at time Ti.

```
%    TRAVEL AGENT

%    LOGIC PROGRAM
     :-op(410,xfxy,'.').

%    OVERALL CONTROL OF DIALOGUE
talk:- default(trip(1),exists),
     default(trip(2),exists),
     default(home_port(1),edinburgh),
```

```
        repeat,dialogue(X),nl,nl,
        display('trips booked :'),nl,nl,
        output(X),nl.
dialogue(X):-
        next_after(0,M),trip_specification(M,X).

%    GATHERING OF TRIP INFORMATION
trip_specification
        (N,tr(d(A),t(B),f(C),to(D),fl(E),
        tr(F)).Ts):-
        discover(date(N),A),discover(time(N),B),
        discover(home_port(N),C),
        discover(foreign_port(N),D),
        get_flight(C,D,A,B,E,N),
        discover(traveller(N),F),!,
        continue(D,F,N,Ts).
continue(Dest,Trav,N,Ts):- nextafter(N,M),!,
        default(home_port(M),Dest),
        recall(home_port(1),H),
        default(foreign_port(M),H),
        default(traveller(M),Trav),!,
        trip_specification(M,Ts).
continue(_,_,_,[]).
get_flight(F,T,D,Ti,Fl,N):-
        fact(ok(Fl,N),yes),
        feasible(F,T,D,Ti,Fl,N),!.
get_flight(F,T,E,Ti,Fl,N):-
        flight(F,T,D,Ti,Fl),
        flight_ok(Fl,N,Con), !, Con = 0.
get_flight(_,_,_,_,_,_):-
        display('no flights available'),
        nl,discover(change,Z).
flight_ok(Fl,N,0):-
        discover(ok(Fl,N),R), !, R = yes.
flight_ok(_,_,1).
feasible(F,T,D,Ti,Fl,N):-
        flight(F,T,D,Ti,Fl),!.
feasible(_,_,_,_,_,N):-
        retract(fact(ok(F,N),X)),fail.

%    MANIPULATION OF FACTS
discover(Lit,Val):- fact(Lit,Val), !.
discover(Lit,Val):-
```

```
    repeat,ask_client(Lit,Val,Con), !,
    Con = 0.
default(Lit,Val):- fact(Lit,New_val), !.
default(Lit,Val):- assert(fact(Lit,Val)), !.
recall(Lit,Val):- fact(Lit,Val), !.

%   COMMUNICATION WITH USER
ask_client(Lit,Val,Con):-
    display(Lit), display(' ?'),nl,
    read(Input), interpret(Input,Con), !,
    not_ask_again(Lit,Val,Con), !.
not_ask_again(Lit,Val,0):- !, fact(Lit,Val).
not_ask_again(_,_,_).
interpret([],0).
interpret(A,B,R):-
    deal_with(A,S), interpret(B,T),
    R is S + T.
deal_with(A.B,0):- fact(A,B), !.
deal_with(A.B,1):-
    fact(A,C),retract(fact(A,C)),
    assert(fact(A,B)), !.
deal_with(A.B,[]):- assert(fact(A,B)).

%   MISCELLANEOUS
next_after(N,M):- fact(trip(M),exists), N<M,
    P is N+ 1, none_between(P,M), !.
none_between(X,X):- !.
none_between(X,Y):-
    fact(trip(X),exists), !, fail.
none_between(X,Y):- Z is X + 1,
    none_between(Z,Y).
output(A,B):- display(A), nl,output(B).
output(_).

%   FLIGHT INFORMATION
flight(edinburgh,paris,jan,morn,f1).
flight(edinburgh,paris,jan,aft,f2).
flight(edinburgh,paris,jan,aft,f3).
flight(paris,rome,feb,morn,f4).
flight(paris,rome,feb,morn,f5).
flight(paris,rome,feb,aft,f6).
flight(rome,edinburgh,mar,morn,f7).
```

A sample session might be:

```
:-talk
date(1)?
[trip(3).exists,foreignport(1).paris,
    foreignport(2).rome].
date(1)?
[date(1).jan,traveller(1).me].
time(1)?
[time(1).morn].
ok(f1,1)?
[ok(f1,1).no]
no flights available
change?
[time(1).aft,date(2).feb].
ok(f2,1)?
[ok(f2,1).no].
ok(f3,1)?
time(2)?
[time(2).morn,traveller(2).fred].
ok(f4,2)?
[ok(f4,2).yes].
date(3)?
[date(3).mar,trip(1).notexists,ok(f4,2)no].
ok(f5,2)?
[time(2).aft].
ok(f6,2)?
[ok(f6,2).yes].
time(3).
[time(3).morn].
ok(f7.3)?
[ok(f7.3).yes].
trips booked:
    tr(d(feb),t(aft).f(paris),
    to(rome),fl(f6),tr(fred))
    tr(d(mar),t(morn),f(rome),
    to(edinburgh),fl(f7),tr(fred))
```

8.6 If...Then... Rules

The application of Prolog to expert systems usually makes use of *if...then...* rules. An expert will generally solve a problem along the lines *if (precondition) then (conclusion)*. The conclusion may in practise form part or all of the preconditions for further queries, in an *if...then... chain.* In more complicated cases, an entire *network* of statements may emerge, of great intricacy. Fortunately, this is just the kind of logical puzzle which Prolog is best at! Even if a solution cannot be provided, a Prolog program may indicate what further information is required in order to reach a solution.

As was discussed in chapter two, there are differences between the logical material implication *if...then...* statements as defined by truth tables which form the basis for Prolog, and the sort of *cause and effect* analysis used by experts.

From the programmer's point of view, there is an advantage in making such inferences explicit. It is that each rule defines a small, and largely independent part of a knowledge structure. Thus, the program is easily updated, further rules may be added without involving previous ones and, furthermore, existing rules may be modified without generally upsetting the program.

If...then... Rules Examples

There are three main forms for an *if...then...* statement:

First, given some precondition or preconditions, a certain conclusion can be drawn. For example: *If the light switch is on, the light is off and the television is on, then the lampbulb is faulty.*

Second, if a certain situation arises, a specified action can be taken. For example: *If the lampbulb is faulty then remove it and test it.*

Third, if certain situations occur then some other situations cannot occur. For example: *If the lampbulb is tested and works, then it could not be the lampbulb which was faulty.*

Consider the rule, *If a car's lights dim and the engine will not turn, the battery may be flat.* Such a rule is quite easily expressed in Prolog syntax:

```
battery(flat):-
    engine(will_not_turn),
    lights(dim).
```

If...then... Rules Exercise

Translate the following rules to Prolog notation:

If the correct radio station is not heard, or the tuning light is flickering, continue to turn the tuning dial. If the correct radio station is heard and the tuning light is steady, stop turning the dial.

If...then... Rules Application

PLANNING CASE STUDY.

The object of a planning program is to start from a description of an initial state, and by prescribed actions, arrive at a required final state. An obvious approach is to specify all of the relationships, and all of the objects of the world for which the plan is being made. As facts concerning the plan emerge, the initial state of the world is progressively redefined, until the final state, or goal is arrived at.

This naive approach has at least two shortcomings however. For one thing, as more and more objects and relationships are considered for larger worlds, listing these becomes practically impossible. For another, every change, no matter how small, requires a description of the new state of the entire world to be made.

A far better approach was implemented by Warren (1974) in his planning program WARPLAN. In this, an incremental approach is taken, where attention is focussed on the initial and final states, and the sequence of changes which are required to go from one to the other. The version of WARPLAN in the following case study is based on that given by Kluzniak et al (1985). In this version, the world description is kept separate from the planning procedures.

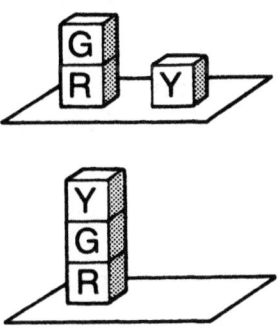

Figure 8.5

The world consists of three cubes and a floor (see Fig. *8.5*). The cubes can be stacked on each other or on the floor. Given a cube C and an object X, (floor or cube) C is initially stacked on X, and C has nothing stacked on it. If a cube does not have another cube stacked on it, it is said to be *clear*. Instead of listing all of the possible arrangements for the cubes, the impossible ones are listed:

A cube cannot be stacked on two different objects.

A cube cannot be in a state where it is stacked on another cube, and that cube is clear.

Two different cubes cannot be stacked on the same cube.

An object cannot be stacked on itself.

In this world, only one kind of action is possible: To move a single clear block, either from another block onto the floor, or from an object onto another clear block. Thus, actions and the relationships between objects implicitly define the objects.

The action for this world is described using the predicate:

```
move(Object_A, Object_B, Object_C).
```

which is interpreted as the movement of object A from object B to object C. In general, any action is subject to three predicates:

```
can(Action, Precondition).
```

allows just one clause for each action. `Precondition` is the conjunction of relationships needed for `Action` to be possible.

A number of utilities are introduced, including & and :. These provide conjunctions, but by varying the precedence number, the need for bracketing is reduced.

```
add(Fact, Action).
```

gives the relationships or `Fact`, added by `Action`.

```
del(Fact, Action).
```

gives the `Fact` deleted by `Action`.

Both `add` and `del` can be understood conversely as the `Action` necessary for `Fact` to be added or deleted.

The predicate

```
impos(Conjunction).
```

states that the conjunction of facts specified is impossible in the given world. Use is also made of the predicate,

```
clear(Cube).
```

indicating that `Cube` is clear.

The operator on is also required to show that one object is stacked on another:

```
Object_A on Object_B.
```

So that objects do not get confused when variables are being use, the predicate,

```
notequal(Object_A, Object_B).
```

is also used.

With these predicates, the fact that *the clear red cube is sitting on another cube* can be written:

```
red_cube on Cube, notequal(Cube,floor),
    clear(red_cube).
```

Some relationships will not be affected by any actions, and these can be precluded by the predicate:

```
always(Fact).
```

It may be desirable to name the initial state using,

```
given(Start_name, Fact).
```

where `Fact` states the initial state and `start` is the name given to it. For example:

```
given(start,
    move(red_cube, green_cube, floor),
    move(green_cube, floor, yellow_cube),
    move(red_cube, floor, green_cube)).
```

The main program begins with a description of the required final state, and an empty plan. At the outset the required final state is checked for consistency, and provided it is consistent, the main routine is called.

As the program runs, successive intermediate states approximate the final state to the initial state. The plan is thus constructed from the goal *backwards*. Obviously actions are required for this. Typically a statement such as `move(green_cube, Object_A, yellow_cube)` would appear, where the prior position of the green cube is not specified. In order to avoid ambiguity in the variable `Object_A`, it is numbered using the built-in predicate `numbervar`. As such variables are instantiated in the backward progress of the plan, they must be preserved.

The main planning routine has the input parameters:

Facts to be achieved.

Facts initially true.

The current state of the plan.

The only output parameter is the final plan.

For each fact of the required goal, the `solve` procedure is called. The two parameters of this routine are:

Facts to be established.

Preserved facts.

The facts may be of differing statuses and different clauses are therefore necessary: The facts may always be true, or alternatively, may be true by virtue of general laws of equality.

Otherwise, the `achieve` procedure is called and suitable actions are sought. This predicate applies an action which must not delete any of the preserved facts, must have preconditions suitable for its application, and must be possible, *ie*; a plan can actually be formulated. If the current action from `achieve` cannot be applied, `achieve` will undo the previous action, and try to put the current action there, provided that the action being undone is not the same as the current action.

There is a predicate `retrace` which removes, from the preserved facts, all of those which could be established from the previous action, but which are not part of its preconditions. In practise, all of the facts added by the previous action are removed, but those which are preconditions are re-inserted.

```
%    WARPLAN-CUBES WORLD
:-   op(50, xfx, on).
add(Object_A on Object_C,
    move(Object_A, Object_B, Object_C)).
add(clear(Object_B),
    move(Object_A, Object_B, Object_C)).
del(Object_A on Object_D,
    move(Object_A, Object_B, Object_C)).
del(clear(Object_C),
    move(Object_A, Object_B, Object_C)).
can(move(Object_A, Object_B, floor),
    Object_A on Object_B &
    notequal(Object_B, floor) &
    clear(Object_A)).
can(move(Object_A, Object_B, Object_C),
    clear(Object_C) &
    Object_A on Object_B &
    notequal(Object_A, Object_C) &
    clear(Object_A)).
imposs(Object_E on Object_F
    & clear(Object_F)).
imposs(Object_E on Object_F &
    Object_E on Object_D &
    notequal(Object_F. Object_D)).
imposs(Object_E on Object_D &
    Object_F on Object_D &
    notequal(Object_D, .floor) &
    notequal(Object_E, Object_F)).
imposs(Object_E on Object_E).
```

```
%     FOR THREE CUBES
given(start, red_cube on floor).
given(start, green_cube on floor).
given(start, yellow_cube on red_cube).
given(start, clear(green_cube)).
given(start, clear(yellow_cube)).
:- plans(yellow_cube on red_cube &
     red_cube on green_cube,start).
:- plans(red_cube on green_cube &
     green_cube on yellow_cube,start).
:- develop('on'), redefine.

%     WARPLAN PLANNER
:- op(200, xfy. &), op(100, yfx, :).

%     Generate and output plan.
plans(C, _):-
     inconsistent(C, true),
     !, write('Impossible'),nl.
plans(C, T):-
     plan(C, true, T, Tl), output(Tl), !.
plans(_, -):-
     write('Can''t do this.'), nl.
output(Xs:X):-
     numbervars(Xs:X, 1, _),outputl(Xs),
     output2(X, '.').
output(_) :-
     write('Nothing need be done.'), nl.
outputl(Xs:X)  :-  !, outputl(Xs),
     output2(X, ':').
outputl(X) :- output2(X, ':').
output2(Item, Punct) :-
     write(Item), write(Punct), nl.

%    Main Planner:
plan(X&C, P, T, T2) :-
     !, solve(X, P, T, Pl, Tl),
plan(C, Pl, Tl, T2).
plan(X, P, T, Tl) :-
     solve(X, P, T, _, Tl).

%    Ways of solving
solve(X, P, T, P, T) :- always(X).
solve(X, P, T, P, T) :- X.
```

```
solve(X, P, T, Pl, T) :-
    holds(X, T), and(X, P, Pl).
solve(X, P, T, X&P, Tl) :-
    add(X, U), achieve(X, U, P, T, Tl).

%    Ways of achieving
%    by extension
achieve(_, U, P, T, Tl:U) :-
    preserves(U, P), can(U, C),
    not inconsistent(C, P),
    plan(C, P, T, Tl), preserves(U, P).

%    by insertion
achieve(X, U, P, T:V, Tl:V) :-
    preserved(X, V), retrace(P, V, Vl),
    achieve(X, U, Pl, T, Tl), preserved(X, V).

%    Check if fact holds in given state
holds(X, _:V) :- add(X, V).
holds(X, T:V) :-
    !, preserved(X, V), holds(X, T),
    preserved(X, V).
holds(X, T) :- given (T, X).

%    To prove that an action preserves a fact
preserves(U, X&C) :-
    preserved(X, U), preserves(U, C).
preserves(_, true).
preserved(X, V) :- check(pres(X, V)).
pres(X, V) :- mk_ground(X&V), not del(X, V).

%    Retraction of goal already achieved
retrace(P, V, P2) :-
    can(V, C), retrace(P, V, C, Pl),
    append(C, Pl, P2).
retrace(X&P, V, C, Pl) :-
    add(Y, V), X==Y, !, retrace(P, V, C, Pl).
retrace(X&P, V, C, Pl) :-
    elem(Y, C), X==Y, !, retrace(P, V, C, Pl).
retrace(X&P, V, C, X&Pl) :-
    retrace(P, V, C, Pl).
retrace(true, _, -, true).
```

```
%    Check for inconsistency with an achieved
%    goal
inconsistent(C, P) :-
    mk_ground(C&P), imposs(S),
    check(intersect(C, S)), implied(S, C&P),
    !.

%    Special utilities
and(X, P, P) :- elem(Y, P), X==Y, !.
and(X, P, X&P).
append(X&C, P, X&Pl) :-!,
    append(C, P, Pl).
append(X, P, X&P).
elem(X, Y&_) :- elem(X, Y).
elem(X, _&C) :- !, elem(X, C).
elem(X, X).
implied(S1&S2, C) :- !, implied(S1, C),
    implied(S2, C).
implied(X, C) :- elem(X, C).
implied(X, _) :- X.
intersect(S1, S2) :- elem(X, S1), elem(X, S2).
notequal(X, Y) :- not X=Y, not X='V'(_),
    not Y='V'(-).
mk_ground(X) :- numbervars(X, 0, _).
numbervars(T,N,Nplusl):-
    var(T),!,T=var/N,Nplusl is N+1.
numbervars(T,N,M):-
    T=..[F|A],numberargs(A,N,M).
numberargs([],N,N):-!.
numberargs([X|L],N,M):-
    numbervars(X,N,Nl),numberargs(L,Nl,Ml).
```

Chapter Nine
PREVENTING AND REMOVING PROGRAM ERRORS

9.1 Introduction

Once a program of any length has been written, it is almost inevitable that it will contain errors or *bugs*. These will not always cause Prolog to generate error statements, but will prevent a program from running correctly, if at all.

Such errors are often due to improper use of syntax. They may also be due to the omission some of the data required for a program's execution. More seriously there may be inadequate, or inaccurate modelling of the original knowledge structure, upon which a program is based. Indeed, the original knowledge structure with which the programmer started may itself be inadequate. Poor programming *style* can also contribute to errors, as well as making them hard to find. Misuse of the search process used by Prolog is also prone to cause errors.

9.2 Errors in the Modelling Process

At the initial stage of modelling, there are a number of errors which can occur. These were all mentioned in the logic chapter, but their relevance to Prolog will now be made more apparent.

The logical connectives adopted by Prolog can easily be misused. On the other hand, apparent cases of their inadequacy may well be due to incomplete or incorrect formulations of the facts and rules introduced at the modelling stage.

Much care has to be taken with *and*, which Prolog takes as being commutative. For example: *Check that the patient is anaethesised and proceed with the incision* does not mean the same as: *Proceed with the incision and check that the patient is anaethesised.*

Similarly, although the word *but* is used as a conjunction, it has a further sense of cause and of degree. *I would have been on time but I overslept* is not the same as *I would have been on time and I overslept.*

If the connective *or* is used, decide whether it is in an inclusive or exclusive sense. The use of the word *or* in: *The equipment may or may not be fused* has a different meaning to its use in: *The equipment should be fused or there will be a danger of fire.* If there is any doubt, it is best to avoid using this disjunction altogether, and to rephrase a statement at the modelling stage if possible, so that there is no room for any ambiguity.

Especial care has to be taken with the *if...then...* connective. For one thing, this does not signify a causal connection: *The poor economic climate has caused a drop in the company's profits* is not the same as: *If there is a poor economic climate then there are poor company profits.* Neither is an accidental or *contingent* connection signified.

A counterfactual states what would have been the case if such-and-such had been the case. In other words, rather than an *if...then...* statement, there is a statement of the form *if...had happened then...would have happened.*

It is easy to mistake a contrary for a contradiction. Therefore when *not* is used, care has to be taken that the negation is actually the alternative represented in the knowledge structure. For example: *The accused was acquitted and is therefore innocent* is not the same as *The accused was acquitted and is therefore not guilty.* This is because the contradictory of *guilty* is *not guilty*, rather than *innocent.*

Remember that Prolog understands *not* in the form *not to my knowledge*, rather than *definitely not.* Consider this example, where two car-part stockists have seemingly given the same information:

Stockist A)   Bolt for bumpstop FORD GT 1976. OUT OF STOCK
Stockist B)   Bolt for bumpstop FORD GT 1976. OBSOLETE

For stockist A, the words *out of stock* relate to a closed world, namely that of the stockist. There is the possibility that the part might be obtained outside that world - at another stockist, perhaps. However, for stockist B, the word *obsolete* is not relative to the world of stockist B, since the part cannot be obtained anywhere.

A term may have a different meaning in different contexts. When modelling a knowledge structure in which the programmer is not actually an expert, there is always the possibility of assuming that the same word always has the same meaning. It is a good idea to ask an expert at the outset, whether there are any such cases of equivocation in the subject terminology. Prolog itself provides an example! Consider: *The argument over the correct number of arguments for the predicate remains unsettled*, where the word *argument* has been used twice, with different meanings.

A sentence may be incorrectly punctuated, so look out for the possibilities of significant ambiguities. If they exist then check that the written meanings are those intended. Consider: *The safety catch must only be released when the warning lights distinctly show green not red or amber and red.* Does this mean green and not red? Is amber and red safe?

Rules can easily be inadequately defined. When they are modelled, the conditions for a rule to hold are sometimes *understood*, but not made explicit. In physics, air resistance may be tacitly neglected when applying Newton's laws. In law, the fact that the statutes only apply to a specific country, may be understood by solicitors, but not stated explicitly.

A rule may be circular, where terms in its head appear in its body. However, this is not to be confused with a recursive definition, where the instantiations of a variable term are different in the head and body of the rule.

9.3 Syntax Errors

Prolog, like most computer languages, is well stocked with syntax error statements. A list of some of these is appended at the back of this book. Just the same, these cannot always be taken at face value. `Last bracket missing` may seem obvious enough: Prolog expects an extra bracket. However the cause of the problem might in fact be that an apostrophe is missing, or misplaced. For example:

```
brother_of('Chris','Leonard)'.
SYNTAX ERROR: Closing bracket missing.
```

Other common causes of errors include putting the wrong number of arguments into a predicate. Using initial lower case letters for variables, upper case letters for constants, and entering . for , and vice versa, are other frequent mistakes.

Most versions of Prolog have *style checks* which will discover mis-spelled predicates. They do this by warning the user when a predicate only appears once. Of course, this means a warning could appear with the introduction of a *new* predicate, or one which *does* only appear once. However, provided a predicate is not *repeatedly* misspelled, it will be brought to the user's attention.

Be careful to avoid inadvertently giving a user-defined predicate, the same name as a built-in predicate. If this occurs, a warning such as `Attempt to modify a sacred procedure`, or `Attempt to alter a built-in predicate` will be displayed. Similarly, attempts to use a name for a predicate which is already user-defined will result in a warning such as `New clause for predicate...` being displayed.

The precedence of the predicates used in a program has to be known. Use of brackets will provide one solution to problems of precedence. However if taken to excess, it is easy to miss one of many pairs of brackets. Prolog will spot this as a syntax error, provided it is not hidden by another syntax error (such as another missing bracket!). Be aware of the precedence of built-in predicates, when formulating clauses and procedures. If necessary use the op predicate to remove any doubt over the precedence required.

In the same way, ensure that the associativity of a predicate, or an operator is as required. The predicate display(predicate) will make it explicit. For example:

```
?- display(x * y - z).
-(*(x, y), z)
?- display(x - z * y).
-(x, *(z, y))
```

9.4 Type Testing of Terms.

To further aid in the extermination of bugs, the type of a term can be examined, whether constant, variable, atom or integer.

The predicate var(term) succeeds if term is an uninstantiated variable. Similarly, nonvar(term) succeeds if term is not a variable, or is currently instantiated.

The predicate atom(term) succeeds if term is an atom.

All clauses containing the predicate term can be listed by using the listing(term) predicate.

The arity and predicate of a stated clause can be discovered using the predicate functor(clause,predicate,arity).

The arguments of a clause can be picked out using the predicate arg(argument,clause,value), where argument is the position of the argument, counting from the left, clause is the clause under scrutiny, and value is the content of the argument of that clause.

Type Testing Examples

Here are some examples of the use of these type testing predicates:

```
?- var(Term).
Term = _1
```

Prolog has instantiated Term to the number 1.

```
?- var(term).
no
```

This indicates that term is a constant.

```
?- nonvar(Term).
no
```

This indicates that Term is a variable.

```
?-  nonvar(term).
yes
```

Here term is shown to be a constant.

```
?-  atom(term).
yes
```

This shows term to be an atom.

```
?-  atom(Term).
no
```

Conversely, Term is not an atom.

```
?-  atom(term_one,term_two).
predicate: atom/2 undefined
```

From this it is seen that there is no predicate for atom requiring two arguments.

```
?-  atom(3).
no
```

Integers and real numbers are not atoms.

```
?-  atom('Janet Jones').
yes
```

Anything placed in single quotes becomes an atom.

Assert:

```
retailer(smiths).
retailer(bhs).
wholesaler(bgm).
wholesaler(direct).
manufacturer(acme).
manufacturer(bosfit).
manufacturer(bgm).
```

Query:

```
?-  listing(wholesaler).
```

This gives the complete list of clauses using the predicate wholesaler. In other words:

```
wholesaler(bgm)
```

and

```
wholesaler(direct)
```

Query:

```
?- functor
   (parents(john,mary,Who),Predicate,Arity)
```

The name of the predicate and the number of arguments will be given for the functor `parents`. Any variables present will also be instantiated to numbers.

```
Who =
_376, Predicate = parents, Arity = 3
```

Query:

```
?- arg
   (2, parents(john,mary,fred), Value).
```

This will give the value of the second argument of the predicate `parents`:

```
Value = mary
```

Some care has to be taken when dealing with arithmetic operators, since they must be expressed in prefix form, before using the `arg` predicate. Thus:

```
?- arg(2, 2 + 3, 3).
no
```

However, the required result will be given if the query is written as:

```
?- arg(2,+(2,3),3)
yes
```

Type Testing Exercise

1. Predict what Prolog will respond for:
   a)   `?- functor([alan,ben],Predicate,Arity).`
   b)   `?- functor(alan,Predicate,Arity).`
   c)   `?- functor(3+2, *, 2).`
2. Predict what Prolog will respond to:
   `?- arg(2,[john,alan,mary],V).`

9.5 More on Type Testing

The predicate `clause(Head, Body)` succeeds if a clause can be found with the specified `Head` and `Body`. If the clause has no body, it will nonetheless be taken as true. Consider the rule:

```
supplies(Outward,Inward):-
    manufacturer(Outward),wholesaler(inward).
```

```
?- clause(supplies(Outward,Inward),Body).
```

gives:

```
Outward = _1  Inward = _2
Body = (manufacturer(_1),wholesaler(_2))

?- clause(supplies(Outward,Inward),
(manufacturer(Outward),Whom)).
```

gives:

```
Outward = _1   Inward = _2
Whom = wholesaler(_2)
```

Further Type Testing Exercise

Apply the clause predicate to the rule, mentioned previously, for joining lists.

9.6 Programming Style

By setting a program out well, many errors can be avoided, or at least their presence made more obvious. As previously mentioned, most versions of Prolog have a style checking facility which will at least help prevent predicates from being misspelt. However the meaning intended for this section goes deeper than this, as will be seen.

By indenting the conditions to a clause, the head and body can be seen more clearly. All of the clauses defining a specific predicate, a *procedure*, should be grouped together with a spare line before and after. For clauses which extend over several lines, it is advisable to start new lines at points which reveal the structure of the premiss most clearly. For example:

```
staff(moss, accounts).
staff(james, accounts).
proposed(james, accounts).
proposed(philips, accounts).

promotion(Name, Dept):-
    staff(Name, Dept),
    proposed(Name, Dept),
    qualified(Name).
```

For a long program, numbering the clauses may be helpful, but if this is done, comment marks must be used unfailingly. Numbering clauses in this way will mean it is easier to make notes and work *off-terminal* developing procedures, while still having a clear record of where any changes would fit into the overall program. Some computers and printers can be instructed to number every line in a print out. However, these numbers will not be consistent between different print-outs of a developing program, and neither will they always appear on the screen of a terminal.

Numbering could be organised in the following way:

```
/* 1 */ staff(moss, accounts).
/* 2 */ promotion(Name, Dept):-
            staff(Name, Dept),
            proposed(Name, Dept),
            qualified(Name).
```

or alternatively:

```
staff(moss, accounts).  %1
```

Here are some further error precautions, to be taken when writing a program:

If two terms actually mean the same thing, then one of them is redundant and should be equated to the other.

There should be frequent comments stating the purpose of all rules, and the likely interpretation of the terms used.

Predicates and arguments should be written using words close to their natural language interpretation. This will save a considerable amount of time and effort in repeatedly trying to remember what, for example, X or Y might have stood for. The extra computer memory involved to do this is negligible. Nonetheless, where a clause is relating to some *utility* which is of quite a general nature, and may not even be specific to the program, such as a user-defined nth_member list predicate, the use of individual letters is more suitable.

The overall structure of a program, should reflect the way in which the knowledge structure itself is *compartmentalised*. Thus, an expert system on abdominal diseases might keep clauses relating to the intestine, separate from those of the pancreas or kidney. Similarly, that part of the program which stores the data may be kept separate from that which holds the routines. Indeed, separate files are generally used in longer programs.

While it may appear elegant and compact to use a single rule instead of several, finding out why such a rule is not working is proportionately more difficult. In the interests of accuracy and clarity, keep clauses and rules as short and simple as possible. As a rule of thumb, do not allow a highly structured knowledge base to have individual clauses containing more than could be *held in mind* at one time.

9.7 Errors due to Search Control

If it is intended to use search control predicates such as cut, sketch a search tree to discover the full extent of the proposed cut. This also applies to the cut/fail combination. There is the possibility that ! is removing the wrong parts of a search or, conversely, it is not removing the parts that it should.

Quite often, cut is introduced as a program is being developed, in order to improve its efficiency, or to avoid loops. When cut is introduced at such times, a major problem can arise: Prolog reads the clauses of a program from left to right and from the top of the program down. As a result, if the relative position of ! within a program is changed, the declarative meaning of the program can be changed. Furthermore this can happen quite unwittingly, since the change made might not itself have concerned !. Thus, when ! is already present in a program, especial care has to be taken with any modifications to that program. If proper care is taken at the time of introducing !, the risks can be minimised. Indeed, Prolog programmers contrast *red* cuts, which are positioned so that any changes to the order of clauses will lead to changes in declarative meaning, from *green* cuts which are positioned so as not to affect the meaning of the program in this way.

Search Control Errors Example

Consider the rule: *If there is alpha emission and beta emission then a proton has been detected.*
Assert:

```
emission(alpha).
emission(beta).
emission(gamma).

particle(proton):-
    emission(alpha),emission(beta).
particle(proton):- emission(gamma).
```

Query:

```
?- proton(X).
X = proton;
X = proton;
no
```

As written here, changing the order of the two rules will not affect the declarative meaning. However, the search continues unnecessarily, having found the only solution. If ! is placed between the conjunctions of the first rule, this can be remedied:

```
particle(proton):-
    emission(alpha),!,emission(beta).
particle(proton):- emission(gamma).
```

Using the same database as before, the following is queried:

```
?- particle(proton).
X = proton;
no
```

Now if this is repeated, with the clauses reversed:

```
particle(proton):- emission(gamma).
particle(proton):-
    emission(alpha),!,emission(beta).
```

The same data is asserted as before, and the same query is made however:

```
?- particle(proton).
X = proton;
X = proton;
no
```

9.8 Debugging

All versions of Prolog have built-in predicates specifically for debugging a program. These are in addition to the built-in predicates for detecting syntax and style errors. The debugging predicates enable a programmer to *freeze-frame* the search process on a procedure by procedure basis. In this way the effect of each and every procedure on the search can be examined. Alternatively, attention can be directed to specified procedures or particular parts of the program.

The *box model* is helpful in order to understand the way in which the debugging predicates operate. Fig. 9.1 depicts a procedure as a box. The terms CALL, EXIT, FAIL and REDO are used to indicate the ways in which the box is currently relating to the search. They are the *ports* of the procedure box. When the search first attempts to match with a procedure, it makes a CALL on that procedure. If matching occurs, the search will EXIT

Figure 9.1

and move on. If matching does not occur, a FAIL occurs and the search will backtrack. After an EXIT from a procedure that procedure may subsequently be returned to. A later attempt to match the same procedure is an attempt to REDO.

The predicate debug switches on the debugger. To get an exhaustive trace of a program, the predicate trace is used. This switches on the debugger if it is not already on, and next time the search enters a procedure box, a prompt will appear to which the user must respond. Clearly, when there are many procedures, there is a need to abbreviate the process in some way. One way is to restrict the type of ports examined. The predicate leash(Mode) does this. A table of the values for Mode is given as an appendix to this book. For example, if Mode is given the value half or 10, only CALL and REDO prompts will appear.

Another restriction on the tracing process is made available using the spy(Predicate) predicate. This causes the trace to stop at procedures in which the predicate Predicate appear. An alternative version is spy(Predicate/Arity). With this, the arity of Predicate is also specified. This version is valuable when more than one predicate with the same name appears, which can be distinguished by their arities. In order to remove such spy-points, the predicates nospy(Predicate) or nospy(Predicate/Arity) can be used. Alternatively, if all spy-points for all predicates are to be removed, the predicate nospyall is used.

The Prolog prompt when a particular procedure is reached, is typically of the form:

```
**(23) 6 CALL: supplies(bhs,_3)?
```

The number in brackets on the left is the *invocation* number. This is a unique number assigned to each procedure as it is first encountered in a search, regardless of whether it is successful or not. The stars ** indicate that a spy point is set in the procedure with predicate supplies. The number 6 indicates the depth to which the search has by then reached. Thus there are six *ancestors* to the exampled procedure. CALL shows that the port involved is the CALL port. The final prompt ? requires some discussion. Prolog expects a coded response to it, in accordance with the following possibilities for further search:

carriage return:
:   Causes a *single-step* to be made to the very next port.

l:
:   Causes a *leap* to be made to the next spy-point.

s:
:   Causes the execution of a procedure to be *skipped*, avoiding

the display of unwanted detail.
It operates at CALL and REDO ports.

f:

Transfers to the FAIL port of the current procedure.
The search is thus on the point of backtracking, from the
present procedure.

r:

Transfers to the CALL port of the current procedure.
The search is thus about to *retry* the procedure.

r(n)

This is an extension of the retry facility r.
Here n is the invocation number for a specific procedure.
Thus, a procedure can be returned to on demand.

g:

The number of ancestors, or *goal-stack* of a the current
procedure is given.

a:

Stops the current execution.

The current state of debugging facilities can be displayed using the predicate
debugging. A typical response would be:

```
Action on unknown predicate: fail
Debug mode is switched on.
Spy-points set on:
supplies/2
Leashing set to half(call,redo).
```

Debugging Examples

Assert:

```
retailer(smiths).
retailer(bhs).
wholesaler(bgm).
wholesaler(direct).
manufacturer(acme).
manufacturer(bosfit).
supplies(Outward,Inward):-
    manufacturer(Outward),wholesaler(Inward).
supplies(Outward,Inward):-
    wholesaler(Outward),retailer(Inward).
```

Now `trace` will be used to provide an exhaustive trace of the search for the query:

```
?-    manufacturer(Who),retailer(Who).

?-    trace.

?-    manufacturer(Who), retailer(Who).
(2) CALL: manufacturer(_1) ?
(2) EXIT: manufacturer(acme) ?
(2) CALL: retailer(acme) ?
(2) FAIL: retailer(acme) ?
(2) REDO: manufacturer(_1) ?
(2) EXIT: manufacturer(bosfit) ?
(2) CALL: retailer(bosfit) ?
(2) FAIL: retailer(bosfit) ?
no
```

Referring to the search diagram in chapter five, the search process initially CALLs on the predicate `manufacturer`, and EXITs with acme. It then CALLs on the first `retailer` predicate but FAILs. Next it REDOes `manufacturer` and EXITs with bosfit. It CALLs on the first `retailer`, but FAILs to match with bosfit. Having been unable to find another case of a `manufacturer` which is also a `retailer`, Prolog answers no.

Here is a more substantial example.

```
join(X,[],X).
join(X,[H|T],L):- join([H|X],T,L).

animal(cat).
animal(dog).
animal(mouse).

sound(cat,purrs).
sound(dog,barks).

chases(cat,mouse).
chases(dog,cat).

canine(Animal):- animal(Animal),
     sound(Animal,bark),
     chases(Animal,cat).
```

Switch to trace:

```
?-    trace.

yes
```

```
?-   canine(Which).
(2) CALL:    canine(_1) ?
(3) CALL:    animal(_1) ?
(3) EXIT:    animal(cat) ?
(3) CALL:    sound(cat,barks) ?
(3) FAIL:    sound(cat,barks) ?
(3) REDO:    animal(_1) ?
(3) EXIT:    animal(dog) ?
(3) CALL:    sound(dog,barks) ?
(3) EXIT:    sound(dog,barks) ?
(3) CALL:    chases(dog,cat) ?
(3) EXIT:    chases(dog,cat) ?
(2) EXIT:    canine(dog) ?
(2) CALL:    write('Which' = dog)
```

Chapter Ten
NATURAL LANGUAGES

10.1 Parsing

One of the original applications of Prolog was to the understanding of natural languages. Sentences of a natural language can be analysed into their grammatical components. In this process of *parsing*, the grammatical structure of the sentence is made explicit and can be checked for correctness. Conversely, given a set of grammatical rules and a dictionary, grammatically correct sentences can be generated.

Although a set of grammatical rules can be expressed informally, this can lead to ambiguities. Accordingly there are formal descriptions for the purpose. One of these is the *Backus-Naur form (BNF)*. Another, which is used in the following example is *definite clause grammar*. In this, the grammar is seen as a set of logical rules which have a syntax which is a simplification of that for Prolog. In a *DCG*, a grammar rule uses the built-in operator `- ->` which is now available on most versions of Prolog. A grammatical rule is of the form:

```
head - -> body
```

For instance:

```
sentence - ->noun_phrase, verb_phrase.
```

says that a sentence takes the form of a noun phrase followed by a verb phrase.

In DCG notation there is a distinction between *terminal* and *non-terminal* symbols. A terminal symbol is represented by any Prolog term. A non-terminal symbol is represented by a Prolog term which is not a list. The head of grammar rule must be non-terminal. Items in the body of a rule may be separated by , which is read as *is followed by*. Alternatives in the body are denoted by ; as usual in Prolog. In this way:

```
noun - -> [boy] ; [house]
```

says that noun is either boy or house.

```
%    DCG REPRESENTATION OF SIMPLE ENGLISH
sentence --> noun_phrase, verb_phrase.
noun_phrase --> determiner, noun.
verb_phrase --> verb; verb, noun_phrase.
determiner --> [the].
noun --> [boy] ; [house].
verb --> [likes].
```

This short program will, for example, check whether the sentence is grammatically correct, and whether phrases drawn from it are also:

```
?-   phrase(sentence, [the, boy, likes, the,
     house]).
     yes

?-   phrase(sentence, [the, boy, likes]).
     no

?-   phrase(sentence, [the, girl, likes, the
     house]).
     no
```

This last query fails because girl is not given as a noun.

```
?-   phrase(verb_phrase, [likes]).
     yes
```

To use the program to generate grammatically correct sentences, a variable is introduced:

```
?-   phrase(sentence, S).
```

```
S = [the, boy, likes]
S = [the, boy, likes, the, boy]
S = [the, boy, likes, the, house]
S = [the, house, likes]
S = [the, house, likes, the, boy]
S = [the, house, likes, the, house]
```

10.2 English to Dutch Translator

The program that follows is an English-to-Dutch translator. (Fowler, 1992). It is only a fragment of a larger program, but it is enough to show a little of what can be done with natural language parsing in Prolog. It takes an English sentence in the form of a list of atoms and prints it out in Dutch:

```
|?-   trans([the,girl,ate,the,apple,and,an,egg]).
      Het meisje at de appel en een ei.
```

```
|?-  trans([the,man,and,the,woman,sang]).
    De man en de vrouw zongen.
```

The program can be divided into three sections: *front-end* predicates, *vocabulary* predicates and *parsing* predicates.

The front-end predicates perform general tasks such as checking the input, the English sentence, for unknown words, passing the sentence to the parsing routines, reporting errors and printing the translation, if one is possible, in *sentence format*.

The predicates which make up the vocabulary database are split into five sections. Each word has a type, and a Dutch and an English translation associated with it, as well as some additional information dependent upon the grammatical category of the word: Number (singular or plural), gender (common or neuter), verb type, tense, etc. This information is used by the parsing routines, and by the front end when checking for the existence of words.

The parsing predicates define the following grammar subset. The symbols in upper case are those which can be replaced directly by Dutch words:

```
sentence -> noun_phrase_group + verb_phrase
verb_phrase -> INTRANSITIVE_VERB
verb_phrase -> TRANSITIVE_VERB + noun_phrase_group
noun_phrase_group -> noun_phrase
noun_phrase_group -> noun_phrase + CONJUNCTION *
noun_phrase_group
noun_phrase -> DETERMINER + NOUN
```

The predicates in this module check that the structure of a sentence presented for translation is one that the program recognises, and translate the sentence into Dutch, correcting errors of agreement at the same time.

Each parsing predicate takes two Dutch and two English phrases as its arguments. Some predicates take some extra arguments which are described further on. The parsing predicates work by attempting to split up an English phrase into specified *subsequences* of the initial phrase. Once the phrase has been broken down to the level of individual words, the Dutch translations for the words are picked up and built up into an equivalent sentence.

In fact the breaking down and rebuilding process works in exactly the same way for both the EngPhr and the DutchPhr arguments, so it can be explained with reference to only one set.

The sentence predicate for example is defined as:

```
sentence(DutchPhr0, DutchPhr, EngPhr0, EngPhr) :-
    noun_phrase_grp(Number,1,DutchPhr0, DutchPhr1,
    EngPhr0,EngPhr1),verb_phrase(Number,
```

```
DutchPhr1, DutchPhr, EngPhr1, EngPhr).
```

If we concentrate only on the EngPhr arguments, this says that sentence is made up of a noun_phrase and a verb_phrase, and that the predicate sentence will be true if there is an English phrase EngPhr0 with EngPhr as the remainder once the sentence (EngPhr0) has been removed.

The subgoal noun_phrase_grp must also be true, where EngPhr1 is the phrase that is left over from EngPhr0 once the English noun phrase has been stripped off, and finally, the subgoal verb_phrase must be true, where EngPhr is what is left over from EngPhr1 once the English verb phrase has been stripped off.

By way of example, if sentence is called with the following arguments:

```
| ?- sentence(_, _, [the,man,has,a,car], []).
```

then this is how its subgoals would look with the EngPhr variables instantiated:

```
noun_phrase_group(_, _, _, _, [the,man,has,a,car],
    [has,a,car]),
verb_phrase(_, _, _, [has,a,car], []).
```

The grammar follows the same method of specification down to its lowest level, thus a noun is given as:

```
noun(NounNum, NounGend, [Dutch|DutchPhr], DutchPhr,
    [Eng|EngPhr], EngPhr) :-
    is_word(noun,Dutch,Eng,NounNum,NounGend,_,_).
```

From this it is seen that something is a noun if EngPhr is what is left over from the English phrase once the noun (Eng) is stripped off the beginning. This is also the point at which actual translation equivalence is established, since the Dutch variable will now be instantiated with the translation for the English word to which Eng is instantiated. At this point the recursion of noun_phrase_group will begin to unwind, and the Dutch phrase will be built up.

If the sentence predicate is given the following arguments:

```
| ?- sentence(D,[],[the,man,has,a,car],[]).
```

It will return:

```
D = [de,man,heeft,een,auto];
```

The following extra arguments are used in the parsing predicates:

The first argument to noun_phrase_grp records whether the subject of the verb is singular, eg. *the man*, or plural, eg. *the men* or *the man and the woman*, This argument is carried over into the verb_phrase predicate to ensure that when a Dutch translation for an English verb is chosen, the correct verb form is picked (for instance, the English *ate* can be singular or plural, but in Dutch the singular form is *at* and the plural form *aten*. Therefore picking the correct translation for *ate* would not be possible without knowing the subject of the verb).

The second argument to noun_phrase_grp is a count to limit the number of nouns in any one noun phrase group. This is to prevent Prolog from recursing infinitely when attempting a match.

The Number and Gender arguments to the noun and determiner predicates ensure that the correct determiner is picked for a Dutch noun. The English *the* may be translated in Dutch as *de*, when used with singular, common-gender nouns and all plural nouns, or *het*, when used with singular neuter nouns. The noun_phrase predicate ensures that the number and gender of a determiner and a noun in a noun phrase match. It also passes the Number argument back to noun_phrase_grp for use in establishing the correct verb form as described above.

FRONT_EN

```
/* Check that all the words exist in the database,
and if they do, then translate English Phrase
(given as a list of atoms) into Dutch */

trans(EngPhrase) :-
    find_unknowns(EngPhrase).
trans(EngPhrase) :-
    sentence(Dutch,[],EngPhrase,[]),
    sent_print(Dutch).
trans(_) :-
    write('Sorry, don''t recognize this type of
    sentence'), nl.

/* Find out if there are any unknown words in the
input */

find_unknowns(EngPhrase) :-
    unknown_words(UnknownWord, _, EngPhrase), !,
    UnknownWord == yes.

unknown_words(Unkn, Unkn, []) :- !.
unknown_words(UnknownWord, Tmp, [H|T]) :-
    is_word(_,_,H,_,_,_,_),
unknown_words(UnknownWord, Tmp, T).
unknown_words(UnknownWord, _, [H|T]) :-
    \+(is_word(_,_,H,_,_,_,_)),
```

```
        write('Unknown word: '), write(H), nl,
        unknown_words(UnknownWord, yes, T).
```

```
/* Print a list of words out as a sentence, with
an uppercase first letter */
```

```
sent_print([FirstWord|RestSent]) :-
        name(FirstWord,[FirstLetter|Rest]),Ucase is
        FirstLetter - 32,
        name(NewFirstWord,[Ucase|Rest]),
        prtp([NewFirstWord|RestSent]).
```

```
prtp([LastWord]) :-
        write(LastWord), write('.'), nl.
prtp([Word|RestSent]) :-
        write(Word), tab(1), prtp(RestSent).
```

PARSER

```
sentence(DutchPhr0, DutchPhr, EngPhr0, EngPhr) :-
        noun_phrase_grp(Number, 1, DutchPhr0,
        DutchPhr1, EngPhr0,EngPhr1),
        verb_phrase(Number, DutchPhr1, DutchPhr,
        EngPhr1, EngPhr).
```

```
verb_phrase(Number, DutchPhr0, DutchPhr, EngPhr0,
        EngPhr) :-
        intrans_verb(Number, DutchPhr0, DutchPhr,
        EngPhr0, EngPhr).
verb_phrase(Number, DutchPhr0, DutchPhr, EngPhr0,
        EngPhr) :-
        trans_verb(Number, DutchPhr0, DutchPhr1,
        EngPhr0, EngPhr1),
        noun_phrase_grp(_, 1, DutchPhr1, DutchPhr,
        EngPhr1, EngPhr).
```

```
noun_phrase_grp(Number, NounCnt, DutchPhr0,
        DutchPhr, EngPhr0, EngPhr) :-
        NounCnt =< 3, noun_phrase(Number, DutchPhr0,
        DutchPhr, EngPhr0, EngPhr).
noun_phrase_grp(plural, NounCnt, DutchPhr0,
        DutchPhr, EngPhr0, EngPhr) :-
        NounCnt =< 3, NewNounCnt is NounCnt+1,
        noun_phrase(_,DutchPhr0,DutchPhr1,EngPhr0,
        EngPhr1),
        conjunction(DutchPhr1,DutchPhr2,EngPhr1,
```

```
        EngPhr2),
        noun_phrase_grp(_, NewNounCnt, DutchPhr2,
        DutchPhr, EngPhr2, EngPhr).
noun_phrase(Number, DutchPhr0, DutchPhr, EngPhr0,
        EngPhr) :-
        determiner(Number, Gender, DutchPhr0,
        DutchPhr1, EngPhr0,EngPhr1),
        noun(Number, Gender, DutchPhr1, DutchPhr,
        EngPhr1, EngPhr).

determiner(DetNum, DetGend, [Dutch|DutchPhr],
        DutchPhr,[Eng|EngPhr], EngPhr) :-
        is_word(det,Dutch,Eng,DetNum,DetGend,_,_).

noun(NounNum, NounGend, [Dutch|DutchPhr],DutchPhr,
        [Eng|EngPhr],  EngPhr) :-
        is_word(noun,Dutch,Eng,NounNum,NounGend,_,_).

conjunction([Dutch|DutchPhr],DutchPhr,
        [Eng|EngPhr], EngPhr) :-
        is_word(conj,Dutch,Eng,_,_,_,_).

intrans_verb(Number,[Dutch|DutchPhr],DutchPhr,
        [Eng|EngPhr],EngPhr) :-
        is_word(verb,Dutch,Eng,Number,_,intrans_vb,_).

trans_verb(Number,[Dutch|DutchPhr],DutchPhr,
        [Eng|EngPhr],EngPhr) :-
        is_word(verb,Dutch,Eng,Number,_,trans_vb,_).

VOCAB

/* Determiners */

is_word(det,de,the,singular,common_gender,_,de).
is_word(det,het,the,singular,neuter_gender,_,het).
is_word(det,de,the,plural,_,_,de).
/* Plural, any gender */
is_word(det,een,a,singular,_,_,een).
/* Singular, any gender */
is_word(det,een,an,singular,_,_,een).
/* Singular, any gender */
is_word(det,geen,no,_,_,_,geen).
/* Singular or plural, any gender */

/* Nouns - singular then plural form */
```

```
is_word(noun,appel,apple,singular,common_gender,
    _,appel).
is_word(noun,appels,apples,plural,common_gender,
    _,appel).
is_word(noun,auto,car,singular,neuter_gender,
    _,auto).
is_word(noun,autos,cars,plural,neuter_gender,
    _,auto).
is_word(noun,ei,egg,singular,neuter_gender,
    _,ei).
is_word(noun,eieren,eggs,plural,neuter_gender,
    _,ei).
is_word(noun,huis,house,singular,neuter_gender,
    _,huis).
is_word(noun,huizen,houses,plural,neuter_gender,
    _,huis).
is_word(noun,jongen,boy,singular,common_gender,
    _,jongen).
is_word(noun,jongens,boys,plural,common_gender,
    _,jongen).
is_word(noun,man,man,singular,common_gender,
    _,man).
is_word(noun,mannen,men,plural,common_gender,
    _,man).
is_word(noun,meisje,girl,singular,neuter_gender,
    _,meisje).
is_word(noun,meisjes,girls,plural,neuter_gender,
    _,meisje).
is_word(noun,vrouw,woman,singular,common_gender,
    _,vrouw).
is_word(noun,vrouwen,women,plural,common_gender,
    _,vrouw).

/* Transitive Verbs - singular then plural form */

is_word(verb,at,ate,singular,past,trans_vb,eten).
is_word(verb,aten,ate,plural,past,trans_vb,eten).
is_word(verb,heeft,has,singular,present,trans_vb,
    hebben).
is_word(verb,hebben,have,plural,present,trans_vb,
    hebben).
is_word(verb,zag,saw,singular,past,trans_vb,zien).
```

```
is_word(verb,zagen,saw,plural,past,trans_vb,zien).

/* Intransitive Verbs - singular then plural form
*/
is_word(verb,loopt,walks,singular,present,
    intrans_vb,lopen).
is_word(verb,lopen,walk,plural,present,
    intrans_vb,lopen).
is_word(verb,zong,sang,singular,past,
    intrans_vb,zingen).
is_word(verb,zongen,sang,plural,past,
    intrans_vb,zingen).

/* Conjunction */

is_word(conj,en,and,_,_,_,en).
```

Chapter Eleven
PHILOSOPHICAL ISSUES

11.1 Introduction

There are two philosophical issues discussed in this chapter. First, what does it mean for a computer to have intelligence and to think? In particular, is Prolog an *artificial intelligence language*, as widely claimed? Second, how does the information given to and provided by the computer relate to the real world? As a philosopher of science might put it: How is *empirical meaning* and significance given to a computer program? In particular, does Prolog fare any better than other languages in this respect?

11.2 Machine Intelligence

The first discussions of the question: *Can computers think?* date back to Turing (1942). Dreyfus (1972) felt that there were four kinds of knowledge. The first two types were completely explicit and situation independent. He proposed that a computer could satisfactorily deal with these. Examples would include spell-checking and simple games, where rules could be given which coped with all eventualities. The third category was similar to these, except for the increased complexity of real-life situations to be programmed. Although the procedures to be handled by the computer were finite, they were too involved for any computers which could actually be built. The fourth category covered the situation in which meaning and situation were not explicit. Such a situation, it was held, a computer could not in principle deal with. Consider the inventive use of metaphor and analogy which is a regular feature of human communication. Here the words used do not relate directly to the situation under consideration. Yet it is often the use of metaphor and analogy which most vividly communicates a thought from one person to another.

Almost certainly, Dreyfus had in mind, computing where rules were given by the programmer, and which the computer followed unfailingly. Most computer languages, including Prolog, fall into this category. To take an example from physics: A computer can readily be programmed to use concepts such as mass, force, length, velocity and acceleration within the laws of physics. It could do this for a wide variety of situations, as requested by the user. However, it is not expected that a computer program actually discover the fundamental concepts and laws of physics. Nonetheless, there is in principle no impossibility about defining a program which will systematically search for such laws, given the appropriate *raw* data. The writers have indeed heard of research work along these lines (Balzer 1991).

It is helpful to distinguish between the action and behaviour of an intelligence. In other words, between the intended act and what is observed to happen. A computer intelligence should at least be *behaviour specific*. It should provide the answers which would have been expected from a competent expert in the field. Indeed, is it reasonable to expect more? Not all experts would approach a given conclusion by the same route, nor think about a problem in the same way.

Turing devised a test for distinguishing between the behaviour of a human and a computer: A human and a computer are set the same task, namely of making conversation through a computer terminal, to another person. If this person cannot distinguish between the computer and the human, the computer is recognised as behaving with human intelligence.

Because this test is performed using a natural language, it is very biased. Perhaps if the natural language were *pruned* so as to remove some of its vagaries and ambiguities, Prolog might yet meet this challenge. Just the same, it is difficult to see how to design a program which not only understood, say, humour, but could create its own. How could there be a program which would understand emotions such as anger and sadness? In response to this one might counter that professional playwrights arouse such emotions in their audience, without necessarily being so affected themselves.

It may be that normal serial computers will never be able to approach the flexibility and inventiveness of human thinking. There may be something about the architecture of the brain, or its varying biochemical composition, which precludes this. Nonetheless, one should not forget that other types of *computer* such as *neural networks*, which have a design closer to that of the brain have already been shown to handle applications such as visual recognition with great versatility.

Prolog programs do not lack learning power however, as some of the examples of this book illustrate. Essentially Prolog programs provide a means for making logical deductions according to the rules and knowledge already given. Abstractive and modelling skills are absent.

Clearly, a Prolog expert system can only mimic certain aspects of intelligent human behaviour. It seems probable that rule-driven programs cannot, in principle, promise the flexibility of the human brain. However, this does not diminish the need for rule-driven programs, where definite behaviour according to well established rules is necessary. It would be foolish to design a missile which had the ability to change its mind about bombing another country. Imagine if it decided it didn't like its creators!

11.3 Empirical Significance

At least between philosophers, there has been much controversy for the greater part of this century about the relation between a scientific theory and the real or *empirical* world. Some of the fruits of this debate are relevant to the question of the empirical significance of computer languages, and specifically Prolog. The programs for a computer are *knowledge structures* to a greater or lesser extent, and face at least some of the same questions of empirical significance as do scientific theories. The input and output to and from a computer, using whatever language, has to relate to the real world that the program is dealing with.

For all of the contemporary activity in computing, it is rare that these vital links in the chain to the real world are examined. It is likely that Prolog makes connections with the real world in a much more secure way than other languages. This is because the data is structured, and forms a *picture* of the real world. In contrast, most other languages use data as singular isolated facts each of which has to correspond to some object in the real world.

A related question is whether it is possible to express a scientific theory or a knowledge structure in predicate logic. Throughout this book there have been examples of this process being carried out, so why should there be any doubt? One problem concerns the formal apparatus of predicate logic. A heroic attempt by Woodger (1959) to put the first law of Mendelian genetics into first order predicate logic, resulted in an unwieldy and opaque edifice. Even expressing arithmetic in predicate logic is at best long-winded, so what chance is there for larger knowledge structures? Well, it is not necessary to reconstruct all of the functions and relations within a knowledge structure, using the full symbolic apparatus of predicate logic. For example, mathematical functions can be kept close to their standard notation and evaluated in the most convenient way. This is effectively what Prolog does, having built-in predicates to deal with functions which would be difficult to formulate and evaluate in predicate logic.

Neither is the idea of defining a set of rules for a knowledge structure without drawbacks. While aspects of a theory are thus made clearer, the importance of one rule relative to another is obscured. For example, if a set of rules is given for maintaining a bicycle, the importance of correct tyre pressure is less than that of securing the front wheel. Again, the need to settle on a particular vocabulary prevents a knowledge structure from developing in a direction which would require a new vocabulary. This may happen when there is a foundational change of theory. In moving from Newtonian to

Einsteinian physics, the term *mass* takes a fundamental change of meaning. Rules asserted using one meaning of the term cannot simply be applied to the term with its new meaning.

Returning to the problem of relating such a set of rules to the real world. This issue has traditionally been part of subject matter for *logical positivism*, or *logical empiricism*, which has provided its most thoroughly thought-out account. The starting point for this view was that many of the issues talked about by philosophers were meaningless. If a philosopher says *God exists because He is everywhere*, does this have any meaning? By logical analysis, positivists hoped to eliminate many of the questions raised by philosophers as *unanswerable*. Central to this aim was the idea that a proposition should be *verifiable* by recourse to the real empirical world. However universally quantified propositions are at best *falsifiable*. Thus, *all swans are white* can not in practise be verified, since no matter how many swans have been seen, there may still be more and one of them may not be white. On the other hand, once a swan is seen which is not white, the proposition is *falsified*. So how can universal statements be verified by recourse to the real world?

According to logical positivism, a *synoptic* approach to the study of science should be taken, by reflecting on the foundations of a science in a process of *logical reconstruction*. Knowledge is to be considered as propositional and communicable within a society by language. Truth of factual statements consists in the following: A one-one, or at least many-one correspondence, of the words, names and predicates of a sentence with the objects, properties and relations denoted by them. There is thus an abstract relation of *correspondence* between terms or collections of terms and what they represent in the real world. Terms which can not be connected to the real world in this way are *meaningless*.

Another problem then arose, as it was found that few terms could be connected, in the required way, to the real world. This is due to the *context-* or *theory-dependence* of terms. For instance, to ascribe empirical meaning to *electron* requires a knowledge of theories which use the term. It is not possible to directly point to an electron and say *that's an electron*. Indeed, for quantum physics the electron is regarded as a wave, while for vacuum physics usually as a particle.

In fairness, many of the early shortcomings were dealt with by the positivists themselves. Just the same, there is the impression that their position could only be saved by introducing increasingly complicated concepts which become ever more difficult to understand. At least one major difficulty remains unresolved: Logical positivists divided the vocabulary of a language into *observational* and *theoretical* terms. *Correspondence rules* were postulated to connect the observational and theoretical terms and thus provide empirical significance for the latter. This meant, however, that the correspondence rules must be part observational and part theoretical. It can be shown by the same logical principles upon which the positivists rely, that if it is allowed that there is a correspondence rule for some term, it renders all terms empirically significant, whether or not correspondence rules have been explicitly stated for them. The technicalities of this proof are beyond the scope of this book. In short, on the positivist account, any knowledge base guarantees its own empirical significance.

Alternatives to logical empiricism have had an *historical*, *psychological* or *sociological* perspective. If there has been a common methodology, it was to make case studies of particular scientific theories in a nonformal way. A recurrent doctrine has been that of the theory-dependence of the terms of a theory, mentioned previously as a problem for logical positivism. However theory dependence of terms leaves two theories *incomparable* since the terms of one theory do not share their meaning with those of another. On this account, no two theories could contradict each other. Yet a science evolves partly by the removal of one theory in favour of another. Furthermore, the principles of a theory apparently become true because of the theory and without recourse to the empirical world. Since all terms are defined by their theories, no observations could be made which would *refute* those theories.

Structuralism (see Sneed 1971) provides a formal model-theoretic and set-theoretic means for making sense of the idea that a group of scientists may hold one and the same theory despite changing and varying opinions. In this way a theory may be *immune* to falsification. The fact is that scientists will not give up a theory because of a limited number of failures, but will *adapt* it. The empirical links of a scientific theory are thus more tenuous than might have been thought. Scientific theories are not copies of reality. They are abstractions from reality and as such only approximations to it. It is understandable that such approximations will need to be improved upon as knowledge of a subject area improves. Looked at from this perspective, it seems unreasonable to think that the original version of a theory, based on early limited experiences should remain the same for all time. According to structuralism, empirical structures cannot *in advance* be seen as subsumable under a particular theory, but they can be tested as such. Even if they do not fit, the theory may be *specialised* for a new domain.

There also a *holism* to this account. Because of the set theoretic and model theoretic syntax used, a *picture* of the entire empirical structure under study is provided. This makes it possible to give meaning to a theory not on a term by term basis, but rather through interpretation of the overall structure of the knowledge base.

In practise, computer programs evidently gain acceptable empirical significance. Most computer languages, which handle data on a piecemeal basis, gain empirical meaning term by term. This is essentially the view which logical positivism prescribes. The reason that the positivist failings discussed earlier are not evident here, is probably that the interpretation of the program is substantially supported by explanations to the user from the programmer. Prolog on the other hand, makes the *structure* of the data base explicit. Thus the programmer has less need to add such explanations for the user. Ideally, the data structures of a Prolog program are *isomorphic* with the structures of the real world which the programmer is attempting to model or at least to an abstraction of them. Much of this book has been dedicated to what happens when this is not the case and procedural aspects concerning the computing process itself get in the way. Hopefully as logical programming and Prolog improve, the structure of their programs will more closely picture available models of the real world.

Chapter Twelve
PARALLEL PROCESSING
PROLOG

12.1 Parallel Processing

In 1945, von Neumann wrote about the architecture of the digital computer. Many advances in the hardware of the computer have been made since then. Nonetheless to varying degrees, all computers still have a fundamental drawback in their architecture, which has been called the *von Neumann bottleneck*.

Given that a computer has a central processor and a data store, these can be thought of as connected by a single channel along which information flows. There is thus the inherent possibility for congestion as more and more data has to be handled. Traditionally, computers have been developed with faster and faster processing speeds in order to minimise this problem. This does not remove the fundamental shortcoming of such an architecture, however. Many schemes have been proposed and used as attempts to solve the above problem by having more than one processor, more than one data store and/or more than one channel between these. Such alternatives are generally termed *parallel processors*. Information is processed in *parallel*, as well as sequentially as in a conventional computer. In fact, there are four possible architectures in this respect: The von Neumann machine has a single processor and a single data store. There could also be multiple processors and a single data store. Again there is the possibility of a single processor and multiple data stores. The general solution of the von Neumann problem is, however, to use more than one processor and more than one data store with as many connecting channels as required.

Not all computer applications will benefit from parallel processing. Moreover, converting a language and programs written in that language from sequential to parallel processing is not a trivial task. The additional flexibility provided by such architecture carries with it the necessity for additional controls. The effort is considered worthwhile for logic programming languages which are generally expected to benefit from parallel search strategies, and a number of languages have already been developed to this end. In particular, there are versions of Prolog which are now available for use on parallel processors.

12.2 Parallel Processing for Prolog

At the end of chapter three, in discussing computation rules, it was mentioned that other strategies than a *depth-first* one were potentially of value. In particular, *breadth-first* search was mentioned. Despite the advantages that this might offer, this idea was not pursued on account of the difficulties in implementation on a sequential machine. In this chapter, a more liberal approach to search strategies can be taken.

It must be understood that we can only sketch the range of parallel Prolog here. Also, it can be argued that rather than develop new parallel Prologs, ordinary Prolog should be adapted to run on parallel processors. This might make for less problems of incompatibility.

The efficiency of a Prolog program might be improved by using parallel processing. In principle, if ten processors were used instead of one, the time taken to execute a program would be reduced by an order of magnitude. For some longer and more complex programs, such savings could be critical. Efficiency could also be improved in the sense that unfruitful searching can be avoided. For example, consider the sorting program:

```
sort(X,Y):- permutation(X,Y),order(Y).
```

According to this, list X is sorted from list X if and only if Y is a permutation of X generated by the predicate `permutation`, and Y is ordered by a predicate `order`. In a depth-first search, permutations of X will be generated, whether or not there is a corresponding ordering for Y. On the other hand, if `permutation(X,Y)` and `order(Y)` are executed in parallel, if `order(Y)` fails, `permutation(X,Y)` will not be called.

More important than improvements in efficiency though, are improvements in the *completeness* of a parallel search. By completeness is meant that the empty clause is eventually derived if inconsistency exists (see chapter three). Ordinarily, Prolog uses a form of search strategy in which when the resolved clause of two given clauses is formed, one of the original clauses can itself be a resolved clause. Such a strategy provides an incomplete search: There is the potential for infinite loops. Also, changing the relative position of clauses in the program as written can affect the declarative meaning of the program. For example, if `integer` is defined by:

```
integer(s(X)):- integer(X).
integer(0).
```

The first clause will recurrently unify indefinitely. Instead the clauses must be written:

```
integer(0).
integer(s(X)):- integer(X).
```

Such difficulties should not arise in parallel processing, since the two clauses are processed simultaneously.

So, the ideals of improved efficiency and completeness can be pursued better using parallel processing. Unfortunately, these aims are to some extent opposing. As the efficiency of a program is improved, the completeness is impaired and vice versa. Efficiency is generally achieved by restricting the search, with the inherent risk of incomplete searching that this brings. To put matters into perspective, though, Prolog itself is not complete, and it is usually accepted that a proposed parallel logic programming language need only be ât least as complete as ordinary Prolog.

One way of making a 'complete' search strategy would be to ensure that when two clauses are resolved, both are input clauses, that is to say they are not themselves the result of a resolution. This is known as *linear input resolution*. Prolog uses a restricted form of this. Another form of complete search is the *linear resolution* strategy. In this, a given set of clauses is divided into two groups such that the clauses in one group are not allowed to resolve with those of the other.

There are a number of types of parallel search strategy or *parallelism*. In *or-parallelism*, (see Fig. 3.1), the goals in the search tree C and F are searched simultaneously. The search then continues to goals D, E, G and H. If a successful match for a single goal is found at (say) H, this search will have been quicker than that of a normal sequential Prolog search. In fact, if the successful match is anywhere except along the leftmost branches, the or-parallel search will be quicker than for a left-recursive Prolog. In general, it could be claimed that such a strategy would usually provide improved efficiency.

There are a number of drawbacks to or-parallelism however. It is evident from Fig 3.1 that as the depth of the search increases, the number of goals to be considered simultaneously will increase exponentially. Ultimately, insufficient processors may be available to carry out the processing. In fact, when a single goal is sought, there will rarely be the need for a complete search of the tree. Usually, a left- or right- recursive search would find the solution without an exhaustive search. There is thus unnecessary searching in almost all applications of or-parallelism to finding a single goal. There is also a problem of access to the facts and rules of the database, for which there will be competition between processors.

In *and-parallelism*, clauses involving the same predicate are searched simultaneously. In this way, the search is made relative to the goal at hand. It is however necessary to ensure that any instantiations given to a variable which is the argument of a predicate in one branch of a search tree match that given in another branch which is simultaneously being searched. Methods of coordination between the searching of different branches are thus required.

Stream-parallelism is a form of and-parallelism with a sequential element to it. First, all matches for the first term in the body of a rule are found. The result is sent to the processor for the second term of that rule body and so on. Because of the part-sequential nature of stream parallelism, it suffers to an extent from the Turing bottleneck problem mentioned earlier.

It is helpful to make use of a concept of *non-determinism* in a search strategy, recognised by Kowalski (1979). In this, if several alternative clauses could unify with a given goal, the clause to be tried is left unspecified. There are two kinds of such non-determinism. For *don't care* non-determinism, once a solution is found, alternative clauses are not tried. For *don't know* non-determinism, all alternative clauses are tried, regardless of success.

It can be shown that a logic programming language must be don't know non-deterministic to be complete. An example of such a system was designed by Pollard (1981). This gave an unrestrained and-parallel and or-parallel execution of Horn clauses. There is a need for a *checker* with this system to ensure that when variables are shared by goals in different branches, there is no inconsistency.

Logic programmming systems which only used or-parallelism have been built, but as would be expected from what has been said previously about or-parallelism, there is a problem with search space. There is also a problem with completeness with practical systems.

A satisfactory level of completeness with improved efficiency has been obtained in systems such as *IC-Prolog* and *Delta-Prolog*. These feature a global backtracking scheme and use stream and-parallelism. Other such systems have been developed which use some parallelism for efficiency while offering completeness at least to the level of Prolog.

If don't know non-determinism is sacrificed, efficiency can be taken more seriously. Thus, an idea of *guarded commands* can be used with don't care non-determinism. In *Relational Language*, so called *guarded Horn clauses* are used. A sequential *and* operator is introduced :. Goals after this in the *body* of a clause cannot be resolved until all of the goals before : in the *guard* of the clause have been resolved. The operator : also causes the execution of alternate clauses for the same predicate to be stopped, if a given clause has resolved the goals in its guard successfully.

The effect of : on a parallel logic programming system is as follows. For and-parallelism, all goals inside the guard and the body are resolved in parallel, while the guard is executed sequentially before the body. For or-parallelism, only guards of alternate clauses are executed in parallel. If one of these successfully reduces the goals in its guard, all alternative clauses are discarded. Such languages are known as *committed choice non-deterministic languages*.

As has already been said earlier in this book, it is necessary to introduce control mechanisms for ordinary Prolog in order to improve efficiency. This is also the case with parallel logic programming languages. There can be corresponding disadvantages in that the declarative meaning of a program is affected. One of the controls necessary for parallel logic programming languages is the need to synchronise the execution of goals. For and-parallel execution, a variable which is shared by more than one goal provides the synchronisation. Efficiency of the synchronisation process can be improved by using *read only* and *mode* annotations to such variables. In these, the system can recognise a variable as an *input port* and suspend its unification until it is bound to other goals. Such approaches have the disadvantage that much of the declarative meaning of a program can be lost by the inclusion of these extralogical devices. One way round the problem is to have an algorithm which analyses the dependency of variables during the run of the program. In this way, for example, Prolog clauses may be compiled into *execution graphs* and the analysis of the search tree simplified.

A recent parallel programming language for Prolog is *P-Prolog* (Yang 1992). This uses guarded Horn clauses while retaining don't know non-determinism. In this, the concept of an *exclusive* relation of Horn clauses is introduced to provide the synchronisation method.

Clearly, parallel processing in Prolog is still at an innovative phase. Nonetheless, as parallel processors become more economically priced they will be more widely used. There can be little doubt that today's computer sciences students will have to meet such challenges, as the computer scientists of tomorrow. We hope that in this chapter we have at least provided a useful introduction .

Appendix One
DICTIONARY OF BUILT-IN PREDICATES

abolish(F,A)

> Removes all clauses containing functor F with arity A.

arg(I,S,A)

> Succeeds if statement S has I'th argument A.

assert(C)

> Asserts clause C at end of a program.

asserta(C)

> Assert clause C at beginning of a program.

assertz(C)

> Assert clause C at end of a program.

atom(T)

> Succeeds if term T is an atom.

atomic(T)

> Succeeds if term T is an atom or an integer.

call(G)

> Calls up goal G.

clause(H,B)

> Causes H and B to be matched with the head and body of an existing clause in a database.

constant(T)

> Succeeds if term T is an atom or an integer.

consult(F)

> Loads a program with filename F.

`consult(user)`

        Allows assertions to be made from the user terminal.

`display(L)`

        Displays the current program listing on screen.

`display(T)`

        Displays the term T on screen.

`exit`

        Ends Prolog session.

`eof`

        End of file - used after making assertions to return to the query prompt.

`fail`

        Always fails. (Used in search control.)

`functor(S,F,A)`

        Succeeds if statement S has principal functor F, and argument A.

`get(C)`

        Takes the next printable character from the current input file.

`get0(C)`

        Takes the next character from the current input file.

`integer(T)`

        Succeeds if term T is an integer.

`listing`

        Lists current program on screen.

`listing(P)`

        Lists only the predicates P on screen.

`name(A,L)`

        Lists the characters in argunent A in ASCII code.

`nl`

        Starts a new line.

`nonvar(T)`

        Succeeds if term T is not a variable.

`not`

        Prefix operator for negation.

```
not(G)
```
> Fails if the goal G succeeds.

```
put(C)
```
> Sends the character C to the current output file.

```
read(T)
```
> Succeeds if T is the next term from the current input file.

```
reconsult(F)
```
> Similar to consult, but causes F to supersede any existing clauses for the same predicate.

```
repeat
```
> Allows search to continue to succeed.

```
save(F)
```
> Saves the current program with filename F.

```
see(F)
```
> Succeeds if the new current input file is F.

```
seeing(F)
```
> Succeeds if F is the current input file.

```
seen
```
> Closes current input file.

```
skip(C)
```
> Jumps to character C in current input file.

```
spy(P)
```
> Spies on predicate P in debugging.

```
tab(N)
```
> Sends N spaces to the current output file.

```
tell(F)
```
> Opens the file F for input.

```
telling(F)
```
> Gives current output file the name F.

```
told
```
> Closes the current output file.

```
trace
```
> Prolog prompt for a goal to trace.

```
trace(G)
```
> Traces the goal G.

```
true
```
Always succeeds. (Used in search control.)

```
var(T)
```
Succeeds if term T is a variable.

```
write(T)
```
Sends term T to current output file.

```
!
```
Cut. (Used in search control.)

```
A = B
```
Unifies A with B.

```
;
```
Disjunction.

```
,
```
Conjunction.

```
A \= B
```
Negation of A = B.

```
S == T
```
Identifies term S with term T.

```
S \== T
```
Negation of S == T.

```
I =:= J
```
The value of I is not numerically equal to J.

```
I + J
```
Arithmetic addition.

```
I - J
```
Arithmetic subtraction.

```
I / J
```
Arithmetic division.

```
I * J
```
Arithmetic multiplication.

```
I < J
```
Asserts that the value I is numerically less than J.

```
I > J
```
Asserts that the value I is numerically greater than J.

```
I >= J
```
>   Asserts that the value I is greater than or equal to J.
>   (arithmetic)

```
I =< J
```
>   Asserts that the value I is less than or equal to J.
>   (arithmetic)

```
I =\= J
```
>   Asserts that the value of I is not equal to J. (arithmetic)

```
-I
```
>   Arithmetic minus.

```
I mod J
```
>   (I modulo J.) Gives the remainder when I is divided by J.

```
+I
```
>   Arithmetic plus.

```
R is C
```
>   Makes R the result of the calculation C.

```
=..
```
>   univ. Creates and accesses arguments of arbitrary
>   structures.

Appendix Two
GLOSSARY OF TERMS

anonymous variable/ blank variable.
> The anonymous variable is used when an argument is not necessarily intended to be instantiated to a constant.

argument.
> An argument is the constant or variable which is the subject of some predicate, relation, functor or operator.

arity.
> The arity of a predicate, relation, functor or operator is the number of arguments it contains.

ASCII code.
> ASCII is an abbreviation for the American Standard Code for Information Interchange. It encodes the characters used on a computer as numbers.

assertion/proposition.
> An assertion is a statement which may be true or false.

associativity.
> An operator ¤ is defined as associative if and only if for all a, b, c in an arbitrary set S,
> $$(a¤b)¤c = a¤(b¤c).$$

atoms.
> Atoms are constants, but not integers. In Prolog, they are always written as beginning with a lower case letter unless enclosed in single quotes, in which case anything can be written.

backtracking.
> Backtracking occurs when an attempt is made to rematch a clause.

blank variable.
> See *anonymous variable*.

body.
> The right hand section of a Prolog clause
> $$A :- B.$$

built-in predicate.
> Predicates, relations and operators which are already available within a version of Prolog, and hence do not need to be defined by the user.

characters.
> The upper and lower case letters, digits and signs generally used in communicating with a computer via a keyboard.

clausal form.
> Clausal form is a way of writing the formulae of a predicate calculus which renders them more accessible to mechanical proof.

clause.
> A clause is a fact or rule. In Prolog, it must be followed by . the full stop or period.

comment.
> A comment is ignored by the computer and is present to clarify the program to the programmer. It is written as
>
> /*comment*/ or as % comment

compound term.
> See *structure*.

conjunction.
> A word such as *and* is a conjunction. It is signified by , in Prolog.

connectives.
> Connectives are used to join parts of a statement together.
> Examples are *not*, *and*, and *or*.

constant.
> A constant is the name of a specific object or relationship, either an atom or an integer.

current input/output stream.
> The current input and output stream is usually the computer keyboard and VDU respectively.

database.
> The database is the facts and rules of a Prolog program.

debugging.
>   Debugging is the process of removing the causes by which a program
>   fails to operate as required for reasons of the program.

digits.
>   The digits are usually taken as *0,1,2,3,4,5,6,7,8,9.*

disjunction.
>   The word *or* can be used to signify disjunction. In Prolog it is written

Edinburgh Prolog.
>   Edinburgh Prolog is the *core* form of Prolog upon which other versions
>   are usually based.

fact.
>   A fact is a clause which is unconditional and therefore has an empty
>   body.

file.
>   At the simplest level, a file consists of sequences of characters stored
>   on a medium which is usually magnetic.

functor.
>   A functor is a relation. predicate or operator.

goal.
>   The goal of a particular query is what is to be achieved, the answer, or
>   a suitable matching of predicates and arguments.

head.
>   The head of a list is the first element of the list. The head of a clause is
>   the left hand part of it.
>
>   A:- B.

Horn clause.
>   A Horn clause contains only one positive literal. In Prolog, this
>   translates to a single conclusion drawn from any number of conditions.

inference.
>   An inference is the logical process by which some conclusion is drawn
>   from given facts and rules. If the inference is correct, it is valid,
>   otherwise it is invalid.

infix notation.
>   Infix notation is used when operators are written between their
>   arguments, as is usual in arithmetic.
>
>   *a+b, a<b, x*y.*

instantiation.
> Instantiation is the replacement of a variable by a constant.

integer.
> The integers are the positive and negative whole numbers, including zero; ...*-3, -2, -1, 0, 1, 2, 3.*

list.
> A list is a sequence of elements which generally bear some relation to one another. The list is a basic data structure in Prolog.

logic programming.
> Programming using principles from logic, in which the computer is given facts and rules and asked to reach conclusions. Instructions specific to the way in which the computer runs the program need not concern the user in an ideal logic programming language.

matching.
> Matching is the process by which Prolog searches its database for a fact identical to that of some query asked of it.

operator.
> An operator is a relation or functor. It is generally, but not necessarily written in infix notation.

postfix.
> A predicate, relation or functor is written in postfix notation when the argument is written first.
> $$xP. \quad xyP.$$

precedence.
> The order in which different operators, relations, functors or predicates are to be evaluated is the precedence. It is signified in Prolog by a number, usually between *0* and *2000*.

predicate.
> A predicate is a statement about one or more objects.

predicate calculus.
> A predicate calculus is a logistic system using predicates, functors, relations and operators as well as logical connectives and rules of inference.

prefix.
> A predicate, relation or functor is written in prefix notation if it is followed by the argument.
> $$Px, \quad Pxy.$$

procedure.
> A procedure comprises all of the clauses involving a specified predicate.

quantifier.
> A quantifier is necessary to state the extent of some variable as either existential (some) or universal (all). It is tacit in Prolog.

query.
> A question put by the user to a running Prolog program.

recursion.
> Recursion is a procedure by which the definition or evaluation of some statement can be progressively refined by systematic reference to earlier definitions or values.

resolution.
> Resolution is a rule of inference which assists in the mechanisation of logical proof.

rules.
> A rule specifies something which is true, provided some condition is satisfied. A rule is written in the form $H : - B$, for Prolog, where H is the head of the rule and B its body. H contains the conclusion and B the premisses of the rule.

search.
> The process of goal satisfaction is a search.

semantics.
> The semantics of a language is the meaning given to its statements by recourse to information from outside of the language.

Skolem constants.
> Skolem constants are introduced to remove quantifiers in preparation for proof mechanisation. This process is referred to as *skolemnisation.*

spy-points.
> Spy-points are used to specify suspect predicates of a program in debugging.

stream.
> The sequential flow of data into and out of the computer and its peripherals.

string.
> A string is a sequence of characters.

structure.

A structure is a predicate with various components which may themselves include predicates and further components.

subgoal.

A condition within the body of a rule or compound query.

syntax.

The rules by which the symbols of a language may be correctly used constitute its syntax.

system predicate.

System predicates are built-in predicates concerning the operation of the system.

tail.

The tail of a list is the sequence of elements to the right of the first term.

term.

A constant, variable or structure which can be an argument to some predicate or structure.

truth table.

A truth table indicates the truth values associated with a connective when different combinations of truth values are allocated to its arguments.

truth value.

A truth value is either true or false in the present circumstances.

unification.

The result of successful resolution is unification, the matching of a subgoal with the head of a clause. Prolog, matching is not exactly the same as unification.

variable.

A variable is a *place-marker* for the argument of a predicate, relation, functor or operator. It is instantiated to a constant. Prolog skolemnises variables during a search by giving them number values.

Appendix Three
COMMON ERROR STATEMENTS

`accessing or modifying system procedures`
> An attempt is being made to modify a built-in predicate.

`comma or closing round bracket expected`
> Could be as stated, but a misplaced single quote could also cause this statement to appear.

`<<here>>`
> Used to pinpoint the actual position of a syntax error.

`host will not permit file to be opened`
> Often due to the filename being mispelled, and hence it cannot be found.

`illegal attempt to modify a sacred procedure`
> An attempt is being made to modify a built-in predicate.

`incorrect position for culprit: culprit:atom`
> An atom is misplaced.

`infix or postfix operator expected`
> Typically due to a typing error, maybe a misplaced or missing comma.

`new clauses`
> A clause using an established predicate has been added. The user may not have been aware that a chosen predicate name was already in use.

`operator expected after expression`
> Probably due to a misunderstanding of the type of a given operator.

`Option not applicable at this port`
> Indication that a specified debugging command cannot be carried out.

`SYNTAX ERROR: <<GOAL>> in lines <<INTEGER>> - <<INTEGER>>`
> Points out which goals of the program contain syntax errors.

`The procedure <<PREDICATE>> is being redefined`
> Warns that a chosen predicate is already in use, in case the user is unaware of that fact.

`token cannot start expression`
> A clause cannot start with, say, ,. The keyboard may have been touched inadvertently just prior to typing a clause in.

`unmatched closing bracket`
> Intended to show that a closing bracket is missing, but also appears when, say, a single quote and a bracket have become interchanged.

`WARNING: <<LIST>> - singleton variables in <<PREDICATE>> in lines <<INTEGER>> - <<INTEGER>>`
> One or more variables have appeared only once in the numbered lines. This may be due to their being typed wrongly, or it may be the user's intention.

`WARNING: <<PREDICATE>> - attempt to redefine built_in predicate`
> The user is attempting to redefine a built-in predicate.

`WARNING: The predicate <<PREDICATE>> is undefined`
> A predicate may not have been defined, but as likely as not, it has been misspelled, or given the wrong number of arguments, possibly by omitting the comma.

`WARNING: Variable used once only`
> A variable has apparently been used only once. This may be due the variable being misspelled, or it may have been the user's intent

Appendix Four
ASCII CODES

Character	*Code*
Unprintable	up to 31
SPACE	32
!	33
"	34
#	35
$	36
%	37
&	38
'	39
(	40
)	41
*	42
+	43
,	44
-	45
.	46
/	47
0 - 9	48-57
:	58
;	59
<	60
=	61
>	62
?	63
@	64
A - Z	65-90
[	91
\	92
]	93

^	*94*
	95
⁻.	*96*
a - z	*97-122*
{tab}	*123*
l	*124*
}	*125*

Appendix Five
LIST OF OPERATOR PRECEDENCES

Predicate	Precedence
: -	1200
? -	1200
;	1100
,	1000
spy	900
nospy	900
not	800
.	750
= . .	700
=	700
\ =	700
is	700
=:=	700
=\=	700
<	700
=<	700
>	700
>=	700
==	700
\==	700
-	500
+	500
/	400
*	400
div	400
mod	300

Appendix Six
PROLOG VERSIONS

BORLAND

Borland International,
PDC Prolog, 68 14th St., NW, Ste 200,
Atlanta, GA 30318, USA.

C PROLOG

Edinburgh University,
Dept., Architecture, 20 Chambers St.,
Edinburgh, EH1 1JZ, Scotland.

HUMBOLDT

University of Humboldt, Berlin,
Germany.

LPA PROLOG

Logic Programming Associates,
Studio 4, The Royal Victoria Patriotic
Building, Trinity Road, London, SW18 3SX,
England.

QUINTUS

Quintus Corporation,
2100 Geng Road,
Palo Alto, California 94303, USA.

SICSTUS

Swedish Institute of Computer Sciences,
PO Box 1263, S-16428, Kista, Sweden.

UNSW

University of New South Wales,
New South Wales, Australia.

Appendix Seven
FURTHER READING

BALLARD, D., and C. BROWN. Computer Vision. Prentice-Hall, Englewood Cliffs, NJ., 1982.

BURNHAM, W.D., and A.R.HALL. Prolog Programming and Applications. John Wiley, NY., 1985.

BRATKO, I. Prolog Programming for Artificial Intelligence. Addison Wesley, Cambridge, Massachusetts, 1986.

CHARNIAK, E., AND D. McDERMOTT, Introduction to Artificial Intelligence. Addison-Wesley, Reading Massachusetts, 1984.

CLOCKSIN, W and C. MELLISH. Programming in Prolog, Springer-Verlag, Berlin, 1982.

COELHO, H., and J.C.COTTA. Prolog by Example. Springer-Verlag, Berlin, 1988.

ENNALS, R. Artificial Intelligence: Applications to Logical Reasoning and Research, Wiley, New York, 1985.

FEIGENBAUM, E., and P. McCORDUCK. The Fifth Generation: Artificial Intelligence and Japan's Computer Challenge to the World. Addison-Wesley, Reading Massachusetts, 1983.

GEVARTER,W.B., Intelligent Machines:An Introductory Perspective of Artificial Intelligence and Robotics. Prentice Hall Inc., Englewood Cliffs, NJ., 1985.

HAYES-ROTH, F., D.LENAT, and D. WATERMAN, Building Expert Systems, Addison Wesley, Reading, Massachusetts, 1983.

KOLMAN, B., and R. BUSBY. Introductory Discrete Structures with Applications. Prentice-Hall, Englewood, NJ., 1987.

LINDSAY, P., and D. NORMAN. Human Information Processing. NY., 1972.

MALPASS, J. Prolog: A Relational Language and its Applications. Prentice Hall, Englewood Cliffs, NJ., 1987.

MICHALSKI, R., J. CARBONELL and T.MITCHELL. Machine Learning: An Artificial Intelligence Approach, Tioga, Palo Alto, California, 1983.

MENDELSON, E., Introduction to Mathematical Logic. Van Nostrand Reinhold, New York, 1964.

NEWMARK, J.D., Logic Programming: Prolog and Stream Parallel Languages. Prentice Hall, Australia, 1990.

NILSSON, U., and J. MATUSZYNSKI. Logic, Programming and Prolog. Wiley, Chichester, England.

REITMAN, W. Artificial Intelligence Applications for Business. Ablex, Norwood, NJ., 1984.

SHANK, R. and R. ABELSON, Scripts, Plans, Goals and Understanding. Lawrence Erlbaum, Hillsdale, 1977.

STERLING, L and E. SHAPIRO. The Art of Prolog, MIT Press, Cambridge, Massachusetts, 1986.

WALKER, A. Knowledge Systems and Prolog. Addison-Wesley, Reading, Massachusetts, 1987.

WATERMAN, D. A Guide to Expert Systems, Addison Wesley, Reading Massachusetts,Language as a Cognitive Process, Volume 1, Syntax, Addison-Wesley, Reading, Massachusetts, 1983.

WINOGRAD, T., Language as a Cognitive Process, Volume 1, Syntax, Addison-Wesley, Reading, Massachusetts, 1983.

WINSTON, P.H., Artificial Intelligence. Addison-Wesley, Reading, Massachusetts, 1984.

WINSTON, P., and B. HORN. Lisp. Addison-Wesley, Reading Massachusetts, 1984.

WOS, L., and et al. Automated Reasoning: Introduction and Applications. Prentice-Hall, Englewood Cliffs, NJ., 1984.

WULF, W., et al. Fundamental Structures of Computer Science. Addison-Wesley, Reading Massachusetts, 1981.

ZWASS, V., et al. Introduction to Computer Science. Barnes and Noble, New York, 1981.

Appendix Eight
LEASHING DIRECTORY

NAME	NUMBER	CALL	EXIT	REDO	FAIL
off	0	no	no	no	no
	1	no	no	no	yes
	2	no	no	yes	no
	3	no	no	yes	yes
	4	no	yes	no	no
	5	no	yes	no	yes
	6	no	yes	yes	no
	7	no	yes	yes	yes
loose	8	yes	no	no	no
	9	yes	no	no	yes
half	10	yes	no	yes	no
tight	11	yes	no	yes	yes
	12	yes	yes	no	no
	13	yes	yes	no	yes
	14	yes	yes	yes	no
full	15	yes	yes	yes	yes

REFERENCES

Balzer W. and C. M. Dawe (1986a). Structure and Comparison of Genetics Theories. 1. Classical Genetics. Brit. J. Phil. Sci. Vol 37. pp 55-69.

Balzer W. and C. M. Dawe (1986b). Structure and Comparison of Genetic Theories. 2. The Reduction of Character-Factor Genetics to Molecular Genetics. Brit. J. Phil. Sci. Vol.37. pp 177-191.

Balzer W. and C. M. Dawe (1993). Models for Genetics. University of Munich. Munich.

Boden M. A., (1990). The Philosophy of Artificial Intelligence. Oxford University Press. Oxford.

Clocksin W.F. and C. S. Mellish (1981). Programming in Prolog. Springer-Verlag. Berlin.

Coelho H. and J. C. Cotta (1985). Prolog by Example. Springer-Verlag. Berlin.

Copi I. (1967). Symbolic Logic. Collier-Macmillan. London.

Dawe C. M. (1982). PhD Thesis. University of London.

Kluzniak, F. and S. Szpakowicz. (1985). Prolog for Programmers. Academic Press.

Rowe, N. C. (1988). Artificial Intelligence Through Prolog. Prentice Hall. New Jersey.

Sneed J. D. (1971). The Logical Structure of Mathematical Physics. Dordrecht.

Warren D. H. D. (1974). WARPLAN a system for generating plans. Dept. Artificial Intelligence Memo 76. University of Edinburgh.

ANSWERS TO SELECTED QUESTIONS

Answers to *Traditional Logic Exercise*.

1a) The Jones's may not be like the other people who come to see the cricket match, they may live in the street. They are an exception to the rule and should not have been included in its domain.

b) It is wrong to generalise from three cases to all cases.

2. You will have found from this question that separating contraries from contradictories is not so easy. The sense and context in which terms are used will usually be decisive. Ask yourself whether, given the sense and the domain, the two terms are exhaustive. You will see that by changing the sense and/or domain, either answer can be arrived at. The following are given as the answers usually to be expected. If they differ from your, see if you can find out why.

a) contraries,

b) contradictories,

c) contraries,

d) contradictories,

e) contraries,

f) contraries,

g) contradictories.

3. Here are our answers. I have started with a general property and then tried to separate out the specific features.

a) A receptacle for letters from which they may be taken for despatch,

b) A tool used for striking objects such as nails,

c) A computer which enables natural languages to be processed conveniently as in letter writing.

d) A set of instructions which enables a person to make a computer carry out desired procedures. (When you have learned some Prolog, see if you want to modify this definition).

e) A dog is a four-legged mammal. Here various contingent properties can be added. To say *A dog is canine* would be circular however.

Answers to Symbolic Logic Exercise.

1a).

p	q	p&q	-(p&q)	-p	-q	-p&-q
T	T	T	F	F	F	F
T	F	F	T	F	T	F
F	T	F	T	T	F	F
F	F	F	T	T	T	T

Columns 4 and 7 different. Not logically equivalent.

1b)

p	q	pvq	-(pvq)	-p	-q	-pv-q
T	T	T	F	F	F	F
T	F	T	F	F	T	T
F	T	T	F	T	F	T
F	F	F	T	T	T	T

Columns 4 and 7 different. Not logically equivalent.

2a) exclusive,
b)   exclusive,
c)   inclusive.
4a) T,
b) T,
c) T,
d) T.
6a) $p \rightarrow r$,
b) $-p \rightarrow -r$,
c) $(-p \;\&\; -q) \rightarrow -r$.
8a) not,
b)   invalid,
c)   invalid.
9a) $-p \lor (-q \lor r)$,
b) $-(-p \lor q) \lor r$,
c) $(-(-p \lor q) \lor (q \lor r)) \;\&\; -(-q \lor r) \lor (-p \lor q)$.
10a) $-(H \;\&\; S), -H \;\&\; -S$,
b) $-(\exists x)(Ux \;\&\; Ix), (\exists x)(-(Ux \;\&\; Ix))$,
c) $-(x)(Px), (x)(-Px)$.

Answers to Predicate Logic Exercise.

1a) assymmetrical, transitive, irreflexive,
b)   assymmetrical, nontransitive, irreflexive,
c)   symmetrical, transitive, irreflexive,
d)   assymmetrical, transitive, irreflexive,

e)   symmetrical, transitive, irreflexive,
f)   assymmetrical, nontransitive, irreflexive,
g)   symmetrical, intransitive, irreflexive.
2a)   *Tab, abT, aTb,*
b)   *Fab, abF, aFb,*
c)   *Bab, abB, aBb,*
d)   *Aab, abA, aAb,*
e)   *Rab, abR, aRb,*
f)   *Pab, abP, aPb,*
g)   *Mab, abM, aMb.*

Answers to Rules Exercise.

1.   ```pet(X):- goldfish(X).```
2.   ```edible(X):- apple(X).```
3.    ```schoolchild:-
         human(X),young(X),goes_to_school(X).```
4.   ```gives(X):- takes(X).```

Answers to Queries Exercise.

1a)   yes.
2b)   ```Niece = diane;
      Niece = joanne;
      no```
c)   ```Aunt = mabel
      Niece = diane;
      Aunt = mabel
      Niece = joanne;
      Aunt = diane
      Niece = john;
      Aunt = diane
      Niece = eve;
      no```

Answers to Blank Variables Exercise.

```friend(X):- likes(X,_).```

Answers to Recursion Exercise.

2.    ```route(First_station,Second_station):-
         next(First_station,Second_station).
      route(First_Station,Second_Station):-
         next(First_station,Middle_station),```
```

```
        next(Middle_station,Second_station).
```
Here, the next predicate signifies that one station is the next stop to
another.

Answers to Arithmetic Predicates Exercise.

1.	no,	2.	C =11,	3.	X = 10,
4.	X = 6,	5.	D = 32,	6.	C = 4,
7.	C = 6,	8.	C = 3,	9.	C = 5, D = 2,
10.	E = 18,	11.	C = 5.		

Answers to Arithmetic Programs Exercise.

1.
```
change(Input,N,N6,N5,N4,N3,N2,1,N0):-
    N0 is (Input mod N),
    N1tot is (Input//N),N1 is (N1tot mod N),
    N2tot is (N1tot//N),N2 is (N2tot mod N),
    N3tot is (N2tot//N),N3 is (N3tot mod N),
    N4tot is (N3tot//N),N4 is (N4tot mod N),
    N5tot is (N4tot//N),N5 is (N5tot mod N),
    N6tot is (N5tot//N),N6 is (N6tot mod N).
```

```
?- change(65,2,C6,C5,C4,C3,C2,C1,C0).
    C6 = 1
    C5 = 0
    C4 = 0
    C3 = 0
    C2 = 0
    C1 = 0
    C0 = 1
```
So *65* is *1000001* in base *2*.

2.
```
tri(1,1).tri(I,S):-
    J is I-1,tri(J,T),S is T + I.
?- tri(5,triangle_number).
    triangle_number = 15
```

3.
```
divfrac(Divisor,Quotient):-
Dividend is (Quotient//Divisor),
Remainder is (Quotient mod Divisor),
write(Dividend),
write(' '),write(Remainder),
write('/'),write(Divisor).
```

4.
```
divdec(Divisor,Quotient):-
    W is (Quotient//Divisor),
```

```
            Rl is (Quotient mod Divisor),
            Cl is (Rl* 10//Divisor),
            R2 is (Rl*10 mod Divisor),
            C2 is (R2*10//Divisor),
            R3 is (R2*10 mod Divisor),
            C3 is (R3*10//Divisor),
            write(W),write('.'),write(Cl),write(C2),
            .write(C3).
```

5.
```
    fac(0,1).
    fac(X,Xf) :-
        Y is X-1, fac(Y,Yf), Xf is Yf*X.
    ?- fac(4,Factorial).
    Factorial = 24
```

Answers to write(term) and read(term) Exercises.

1.
```
    class('Johnson', '2A').
    class('Morris', '3B').
    class('Austen', '1C').
    class('Smith', '4F').
    class('Harrison', '3B').
    class('Audley', '1C').
    find_class:-
        read(Input),class(Input,Output),
        write(Output).
    find_class.
    'Smith'.
    4F
```

2.
```
    polygon(5,pentagon).
    polygon(6,hexagon).
    polygon(7,heptagon).
    polygon(8,octagon).
    polygon(9,nonagon).
    polygon(10,decagon).
    know_polygon:-
        write('how many sides has the polygon?'),
        read(Number),
        polygon(Number, Name),
        write('the polygon is a '),
        write(Name), write(' .').
```

Answers to `tab` *and* `nl` *Exercise.*

1.   table:-
            (tab(20),write('Day'),tab(10),
            write('Max. Temp.'),tab(10),
            write('Min. Temp.'),nl,nl,nl,tab(20),
            write('Mon.'),tab(13),write('12'),tab(19),
            write('3'),nl,nl, tab(20),
            write('Tue.'),tab(13),write('14'),
            tab(19),write('4'), nl, nl,
            tab(20),write('Wed.'),tab(13),write('16'),
            tab(19), write('2'), nl, nl,
            tab(20),write('Thu.'),tab(13),write('19'),
            tab(19),write('4'),nl,nl,
            tab(20),write('Fri.'),tab(13),write('18'),
            tab(19),write('6'),nl,nl,
            tab(20),write('Sat.'),tab(13),write('18'),
            tab(19),write('5'),nl, nl,
            tab(20),write('Sun.'),tab(13),write('18'),
            tab(19),write('0')).

    ?- table.
        Day   Max Temp.   Min Temp.
        Mon.   12   3
        Tue.   14   4
        Wed.   16   2
        Thu.   19   4
        Fri.   18   6
        Sat.   18   5
        Sun.   18   0

2.   Menu:-
            write('Which of the following destinations
            are you interested in?'), nl,
            write('1. FRANCE.'), nl,
            write('2. U.S.A.'), nl,
            write('3. INDIA.'), nl,
            write('Please enter your choice here...').

Answers to Lists Exercise.

1.   Foreman = alfonso

        Gang = [bob,chris,derek]

2.   Team = [bert,charles,desmond]
3.   Foreman = alan
      Supervisor = bert
      Others = [charles,desmond]
4.   All = [alfonso,bob,chris,derek]
5.   Foreman = alfonso
      Student = derek
6.   Error; no clause for relation drivers/2

Answers to Lists Operations Exercise.

1.   1,2,5,7,2,3,5,7

Answers to Semantic Networks Exercise.

```
is_in(bedroom,house).
is_in(lounge,house).
..................
is_in(wardrobe,bedroom).
is_in(bed,bedroom).
..................
is_in(coat,wardrobe).
is_in(hat,wardrobe).
..................
```
A rule for the transitivity of is_in can be added if it is felt appropriate.

Answers to Frames Exercise.

2.   Frame: staff_management_meeting
      a_kind_of: staff_meeting
      location: boardroom
      time: one_pm.

      Frame: staff_union_meeting
      a_kind_of: staff_meeting
      location: canteen
      time: one_pm.

      Frame: other_meetings
      a_kind_of: staff_meeting
      location: canteen
      time: one_pm.

      Frame: redundancy_meeting
      an_instance_of: staff_management_meeting
      date: august third

```
    present: owens, jones, bingham, christie.
```
Answers to If... then... Exercise.

```
dial(turn):-
    heard(not_correct_station);
    light(flickering).
dial(stop):-
    heard(correct station),
    light(steady).
```

INDEX

/*...*/ 28
% 28
= 34, 44
\= 44
< 66
> 66
=< 66
>= 66
+ 65
- 65
* 65
/ 65
! 60
, 33
; 33
^ 65
=... 84
--> 131
∃ 17
→ 17
↔ 17
≡, 14
& 12

anatomy 33
ancestor 46, 129
and parallelism 153
anonymous variable 44
antecedent 9
append 29, 42
arg 120
argument

logical 7
  predicate 30
arithmetic 4, 63
ASCII 29, 75
assert 34
asserta 48
assertz 48
associativity 42, 120
atom
  logical 17
  Prolog 28, 80, 120
atomic formula 21
axiom 12

backtracking 55, 128, 150
binary tree 82
body 37, 123, 131, 150
box model 126
bug 28, 119
built-in predicates 29, 64,
  143

call 39, 84
character 28
circular definition 23
clausal form 21
clause 21, 148
closed world 12, 24
comment 28, 124
commutativity 14
completeness 12

compound formula 12
conclusion 7, 9
conditional 33
conjunction 12, 34, 121
connective 11, 33, 54, 118
consequent 9
constant 12, 28, 119
consult 27
contingent 8
contradiction 14
contrary 118
current input stream 74
current output stream 73
cut 59

data structures 4, 34, 81,
  146
database 27
debugging 126
deduction 3, 10
deductive logic 7
definition 8
digit 28
dilemma 9
disjunction 12, 33, 118
display 4
display 43, 120

Edinburgh Prolog 3
element 42, 71, 81

empirical significance 12, 143
empty clause 148
end_of_file 27
equal 42, 64
equivalence 14
exclusive or 9
existential quantification 17

fact 2, 20, 39
fail 60, 126
FAIL 126
fallacy 10
file 4, 79
filename 28
first order logic 21
frames 102
function 17
functor 17
functor 20

general proposition 17
genetics 97
get 75
get0 75
goal 4, 26, 39, 54
grammar 131

head of list 82
head of rule 37, 121, 134
Horn clause 21, 150
hypothetical proposition 10

if...then... 107
inclusive or 9
incompleteness 20
inconsistency 20
inductive logic 7
inference 7
infix 45
input 73, 143
instantiate 17, 33
insurance quote 89

integer 4, 28, 64, 120
integer 148
interpretation 18
intransitive relations 10
invalid argument 10
irreflexive relations 19
is 64

knowledge structures 3, 20, 143

length 85
linear input resolution 149
LISP 3
list 50, 81
literal 21
logic 7
logic programming 1, 7, 21, 147
logical equivalence 14
logical positivism/ empiricism 144

machine intelligence 144
matching 18, 25, 36
material equivalence 14
material implication 14
meetings program 102
member 51
mod 44
modus ponens 11, 15

name 78
negation 8, 22, 33, 118
nl 74, 76
non-determinism 150
nonvar 124
nospy 127
not 8, 12, 33
not 59

op 38, 120
operator 4, 17, 31, 64

or 9
or parallelism 149
output 73

parallel processing 147
parallelism 130
parsing 131
phrase 131
postfix 17, 31, 42
precedence 12, 42, 120
predicate 9, 17, 29
predicate calculus 21, 33
prefix 17, 31, 122
procedure 31
Prolog 1, 7, 21
proof 11
proposition 8
propositional calculus 12

quantification 17
quantifier 17
query 27, 39
question 27

read 74
reconsult 27
recursion 46
recursive definition 8
reflexive relations 10
repeat 61
resolution 23, 150
retract 48
rule 4, 7, 22, 37
rules of inference 12

search 3, 25, 46, 117, 148
search strategies 46, 148
search tree 26
see 80
seeing 80
seen 80
semantic networks 96
sorting 32, 79, 148
spy 127

spy-point 127
structuralism 145
structure 3, 17, 55, 82, 117,
    143
symmetric relations 10
syntax 29, 73, 145

tab 77
tail 82
taxonomy 97
tell 79
term, predicate calculus 8
term, Prolog 46

told 79
trace 127
tracing 127
transitive relations 10
translator 131
true 8, 35
true 61
truth tables 12
Turing test 141

unification 18, 25, 151
univ 84
universal quantification 17

valid argument 10
var 120
variable 17, 28
von Neuman bottleneck
    147

WARPLAN 109
well-formed formula
write 38, 73

yes 33